NATURAL DISASTERS

An informative book for students preparing for competitive examinations

Dr. Sushmitha Baskar
Dr. R. Baskar

UNICORN BOOKS

Publisher
UNICORN BOOKS

F-2/16, Ansari Road, Daryaganj, New Delhi-110002
E-mail: info@unicornbooks.in • *Website:* www.unicornbooks.in
☎ 011-23275434, 23262683

Branch : Mumbai
23-25, Zaoba Wadi Thakurdwar, Mumbai-400002
☎ 022-22010941, 022-22053387
E-mail: rapidex@bom5.vsnl.net.in

Showroom :
- **PM Publications, New Delhi**
  - 10-B, Netaji Subhash Marg, Daryaganj, New Delhi-110002
  - 6686, Khari Baoli, Delhi-110006

Distributors :
- **Pustak Mahal**
  Bengaluru: ☎ 080-22234025
  Patna: ☎ 0612-3294193

- **V & S Publishers, Hyderabad**
  ☎ 040-24737290

ISBN: 978-81-7806-168-9

Edition: November 2011

Printed at : Param Offsetters, Okhla, New Delhi-110020

Dedicated to

Our parents and teachers

Preface

Time and again history has proved beyond any iota of doubt that civilization can exist and flourish only with the full consent of geology. It was rightly stated by US historian Will Durant, as early as in the 19th century, that "Civilization exists by geological consent, subject to change without notice". All the earth processes have been operating throughout the geological history, but these processes are considered hazardous only because they negatively affect us. These are only natural earth processes and there would be no natural disasters, if it were not for humans. We benefit directly from the earth and our survival depends on many of the natural earth processes. However, the same earth can be a dangerous place and our understanding of these natural hazards is important for our continued success as a species. Developing an understanding of natural hazards is the first step towards disaster preparedness and response. In order to safeguard the developmental gains against the natural hazardous events, we have no choice but to learn about the natural processes occurring on the earth in order to predict hazardous and prepare ourselves. We have no control over the geologic process but we can only try to predict and attempt to reduce the hazardous effects to life and property. We need more rigorous scientific research to attempt to understand and help forecast future events. We need to be able to monitor the hazardous events and to be able to quickly communicate the information without any scientific jargon from the scientists to the general population.

Recognizing the need of the hour, the decade 1990-99 was declared as "International Decade for Natural Disaster Reduction" by the United Nations to focus on disaster management planning for prevention, reduction, and mitigation of the natural disasters. Government of India, Ministry of Human Resource Development in its Tenth Five-Year Plan has emphasized the need for integrating disaster management in the existing education system in India. It is absolutely necessary to sensitise about the understanding of natural hazards, right from school children to adults, as our response to natural hazards will depend on understanding the natural processes. Great care has been taken to incorporate relevant case studies and interesting facts to trigger the mind of the students. This book will be very useful for all students preparing for competitive examinations at the graduate and post-graduate level and to anyone interested to get an overview of the natural hazards.

This textbook is divided into six units and covers a range of topics. Each unit focuses on a specific natural disaster theme. The first unit is a general unit and discusses the importance of natural earth processes that can become hazardous to people, understand the basic ideas of risk assessment and prediction for natural hazards, the need for public awareness and the role of different individuals in the society. The second unit gives a basic understanding of earthquakes, its relationship to plate tectonics, effects of earthquakes, prediction and mitigation. Unit three introduces the students to the study of volcanoes and eruptions resulting from these processes, which could be hazardous. In the fourth unit, a description of weather related hazards, like cyclones, hurricanes, tornadoes, thunderstorms, lightening, drought is highlighted. The fifth unit focuses on floods, their occurrence and how they can be minimized and managed. The last unit deals with landslides, the basic processes operating on slopes, human induced landslides, their prediction and management.

One of our objectives in writing this book is to sensitize the younger generation to understand the natural earth processes so they can act to prevent where possible, prepare for the inevitable, respond to in the best manner, and recover quickly from the impact of natural hazards. We would welcome suggestions, constructive criticism of the book so that the future editions can be improved upon.

We thank Dr D. D. S. Sandhu, Vice-Chancellor, Guru Jambheshwar University of Science and Technology, Hisar for his constant support and encouragement. We also thank Dr Rolf Birger Pederson, Director, Center for Geobiology, Norwegian Center of Excellence, University of Bergen, Norway for generous access to computer facilities and total support. We express our deep gratitude to our support from our parents and teachers, without whom this book would not have been possible. We thank our son, Siddharth Baskar for cooperation and giving some great ideas during the entire course of work.

Dr. R. Baskar
Dr. Sushmitha Baskar

Contents

Unit 1

INTRODUCTION TO NATURAL DISASTERS

"Civilization exists by geological consent, subject to change without notice"

US Historian Will Durant (1885-1981)

Time and again humans have experienced that civilization can exist only with the consent of geology. We know that all the earth processes have been operating throughout the geological history, but these processes have become hazardous only because they negatively affect us. These are only natural earth processes and there would be no natural disasters if it were not for humans. The earth is an open system with respect to energy but essentially a closed system with respect to materials. The earth is also a dynamic, evolving system with complex interactions of internal and external processes. While the internal processes are primarily responsible for movement of plates, earthquakes, volcanic activities, the external processes are responsible for the wave generation, floods, hurricanes, tornadoes and droughts. The source of energy of the internal process is essentially radioactivity, whereas the source of energy for the external process is the sun.

We benefit directly and our survival depends on the Earth's resources. However, the same earth can be a dangerous place and our understanding of these natural hazards is important for our continued success as a species. The first step to deal with hazards is to prepare. Thus, for us to have an understanding of the earth processes in which we live, it is important to look at the processes and structures that occur today, and interpret what could have occurred in the past i.e. applying the Hutton concept "Present is the key to the past".

Geo-hazard is a natural earth process that upon interaction with human activity causes loss of life and / or property. Earth processes means natural events that occur within the lithosphere, hydrosphere or atmosphere. Geologic processes affect every living organism on the Earth all the time, but they become obvious only when they affect life or property. Such life or property threatening processes are called natural hazards. Hazard is an inescapable part of life and no one can live in a totally safe environment. A hazard can be defined as a potential threat to humans and their welfare and risk as the probability of hazard occurrence. A disaster can be defined as the realization of the hazard.

1.1 Natural Hazards

The different types of natural catastrophes include: earthquakes, volcanic eruptions, floods, and landslides, severe weather conditions like tornadoes, cyclones and even meteorite impacts.

The best way to face natural hazards is obviously to predict and prepare. The long-term preparations for hazard mitigation are frequently complex and often involve investment of substantial resources. Among the natural hazards, the possible disasters to be considered are:

- Earthquakes
- Volcanic eruptions
- Tsunamis
- Landslides and subsidence
- Floods and droughts
- Hurricanes and tornadoes
- Meteorite Impacts

The relationship between humans and geologic processes is characterised by risk. The risk from natural hazards, while it cannot be eliminated, can, in some cases be understood in such a way that we can minimize the hazard to humans, and thus minimize the risk. To be able to do this, we must understand something about the processes that operate, and understand the energy required for the process. Then, we can develop an appropriate plan of action for minimizing the risk. This is called hazard mitigation.

At times, human actions play a contributory role in influencing natural disasters. Disasters that are directly caused by human activity are called technological disasters, such as oil and toxic material spills, pollution, massive automobile or train wrecks, air plane crashes, and human induced explosions.

Some of the general questions associated with each natural disaster are:

- Where is the hazard likely to occur?
- Why is the hazard likely to occur?
- How often do these hazards develop into disasters?
- How can each type of disaster be predicted and controlled?

1.2 Dimensions of Hazard

The impact of a disastrous event is in part a function of its magnitude (amount of energy released) and frequency (recurrence interval) but it is influenced by many other factors like climate, geology, vegetation, population and land use. In general, the frequency of such an event is inversely related to the magnitude. Small earthquakes, for example, occur more often than do large ones. The magnitude concept is the assertion that there is generally an inverse relationship between the magnitude of an event and its frequency. In other words, the larger the flood, the less frequently the flood occurs. The concept also supports the idea that much of the work of forming the earth's surface is done by events of moderate magnitude and frequency rather than common processes with low magnitude and high frequency or extreme events of high magnitude and low frequency.

1.3 Hazard Classification

Hazards can be categorized as natural hazards and technological hazards. Natural hazards are basically natural processes, which may become hazardous when people live or work in areas where these processes occur. Technological hazards occur as a direct result of human interaction with the environment. They include hazards, which occur due to exposure to hazardous substances, such as radon, mercury, asbestos fibres, and coal dust. They also include other hazards that have formed only through human interaction, such as acid rain, and contamination of the atmosphere or surface waters with harmful substances, as well as the potential for human destruction of the ozone layer and potential global warming.

Table 1.1 General classifications of hazards

Natural hazards	1. Geologic hazards	Earthquakes, volcanic eruptions, landslides, avalanches, subsidence, and impacts with space objects
	2. Hydrological hazards	Floods, tsunamis
	3. Atmospheric hazards	Hurricanes, tornadoes, droughts, and severe thunderstorms, lightning
	4. Biological hazards	Insect infestations, disease, wildfires
Technological or Anthropogenic hazards		Exposure to hazardous substances, such as radon, mercury, asbestos fibres, and coal dust, acid rain, contamination of the atmosphere or surface water

Natural hazards can also be termed as catastrophic hazards when they have devastating consequences to large numbers of people, or have a worldwide effect, such as impacts of huge volcanic eruptions, worldwide disease epidemics, and worldwide droughts. Natural hazards can also be classified into rapid onset hazards – such as volcanic eruptions, earthquakes, floods, landslides, severe thunderstorms which form with little warning and strike rapidly, or slow onset hazards – like drought and disease epidemics take years to form. Each of these disasters has a different space and time signatures (Table. 1.2; Navalgund, R.R. 2001).

Table 1.2 Disaster time and space characteristics

Type	Impact time	Spatial extent
Earthquake	Seconds to minutes	102 – 104 sq.km
Landslide	Seconds	0.1 – ½ sq. km
Forest fires	Minutes to days	101 – 103 sq. km
Floods	Minutes to hours	105 – 107sq. km
Cyclones	Few hours	103 – 104 sq. km
Drought	Months to years	106 sq. km
Desertification	Tens of years	107 – 108 sq. km

Case Studies Of Natural Hazards

The killer earthquake of Bhuj, Gujarat, India

While the entire country was celebrating the 51st anniversary of the Republic Day on 26th January 2001, a devastating earthquake struck the Bhuj area of the Gujarat State of India. The 7.6 magnitude Bhuj earthquake that shook the Indian Province is one of the two most deadly earthquakes to strike India in its recorded history, killing thousands and causing extensive damage to property. One month after the earthquake Government of India official figures placed the death toll at 19,727, number of injured at 166,000, 600,000 people were left homeless, 348,000 houses destroyed and an additional 844,000 damaged. More than 20,000 cattle were reported killed.

Technological Hazards: Nuclear Accidents and Holocaust

Nuclear holocaust refers to the complete or nearly complete eradication of human civilization by nuclear warfare. Under such a scenario, all or most of the Earth is burnt and destroyed by nuclear weapons in future world wars. The word "holocaust" is defined as "great destruction resulting in the extensive loss of life, especially by fire and is derived from the Greek term "holokaustos" meaning "burnt whole". Nuclear scientists predict that nuclear holocaust can end human life and/or modern civilization on Earth due to the immediate effects of nuclear fallout, the loss of much modern technology due to electromagnetic pulses, or extinction events caused by it, such as nuclear winter.

Nuclear energy is the most advanced technology on this planet, but also equally terrifying. Environmentalists have long been fond of saying that the sun is the only safe nuclear reactor, situated, as it is, some ninety-three million miles away. The bridge between nuclear power and nuclear weapons is that nuclear reactor's by-products contain plutonium, which is the explosive material needed to produce nuclear weapons, as well as enriched uranium.

Nuclear Accidents

The first major nuclear accident was reported in America in 1979. In Three Mile Island, America, small releases of the core had melted down and had been let out into the environment causing a total of 200, 000 people to be displaced. The estimated cleanup costs was around $1 billion. Radioactive waste disposal is of very serious environmental concern and careful geological considerations are of paramount importance.

Case Studies of Technological Hazards

The Terrible Bhopal Gas tragedy in India, 1984

A classic case study involving air pollution is one of India's terrible industrial disasters, which occurred on 3rd December, 1984, in Bhopal, Madhya Pradesh. A Union Carbide Company used methyl isocyanate in manufacturing Carbaryl (carbamate) pesticides. On that day all the safety devices failed and there was a functional failure of the vent scrubber outlet. There was a violent chemical reaction in the tank and the pressure built up causing the popping up of the safety valve. The safety valve remained open for more than two hours releasing

50,000 lbs of gaseous and liquid MIC along with HCN and $COCl_2$ resulting in over 30 - 40 tons of methyl isocyanate (MIC) and 35 – 40 kg phosgene emitted into the atmosphere, seen as thick foggy dense gas clouds. The gas spread over the entire region and city, air being the medium. It is reported that about 5000 people died in the disaster and more than 2,50,000 people were exposed to the gas. MIC afflicts the lungs, eyes, skin, respiratory system; gastrointestinal system and is known to cause reproductive, teratogenic and mutagenic effects. The after effects of the Bhopal gas tragedy are seen even today with people and children having genetic disorders. The cleanup of the tragedy costs were approximately 570 million U.S. dollars compared to the cost of the safety devices, which would have cost only 1 million U.S. dollars, if it had been installed before the tragedy.

The Chernobyl Disaster: The world's worst Nuclear Accident

During the night of 26 April 1986, the world's worst nuclear accident occurred at Chernobyl about 130 km north of the city of Kiev, USSR, when one of the four nuclear reactors exploded and burned. It was an example of a major nuclear pollution incident due to human error. The sky over northern Europe and Scandinavia was filled with radioactive material. The official report mentions that the explosion was due to unauthorized testing by its operators and a major flaw in the design of the reactor. Lumps of radioactive material were ejected from the reactor and deposited within one km of the plant. The main plume of the radioactive dust and gas was in the atmosphere; rich in fission products and the living tissue can readily absorb iodine-131 and caesium-137. During the efforts to control the release of radioactive material 31 people died, 200 people sustained serious injuries through exposure to over 2000 times the normal annual dose from background levels of radiation. An estimated 300 000 to 600 000 people were involved in the cleanup of the explosion. A total of about 160 000 people were evacuated in a 30 kilometer radius of the disaster. Later on, a total of 210 000 people were relocated into less radioactive areas. Within two weeks of the accident the radioactive plume circulated over much of the north Western Europe and deposited radioactive materials. An immediate consequence was the contamination of food chain and restrictions on the sale of vegetables, milk and meat. So far it has been difficult to estimate the long-term health risk, notably the increase in fatal cancers, which can be attributed to the Chernobyl accident.

1.4 Effects of Hazards

Hazardous process of all types can have primary, secondary, and tertiary effects.

Table 1.3 Effects of hazards

Primary Effects	They occur as a result of the process itself	Water damage due to a flood, building collapse due to an earthquake, landslide, hurricane, or tornado.
Secondary Effects	They occur only because a primary effect has caused them	Fires ignited by earthquakes or volcanic eruptions, disruption of electrical power and water service as a result of an earthquake or flood and flooding caused by a landslide moving into a lake or river.
Tertiary Effects	They are long-term effects that are set off as a result of a primary event	Loss of habitat due to floods, crop failure caused by a volcanic eruption etc.

1.5 Vulnerability and Susceptibility of Hazards

Vulnerability refers to not only the possible physical effects of a natural hazard, but the way it affects human life and property. Vulnerability to a given hazard depends on a number of factors like

- Proximity to a possible hazardous event
- Population density, construction styles and building codes

•Understanding and awareness of the nature of the hazard

• Early-warning systems, lines of communication and emergency infrastructure

Generally, less developed countries are more vulnerable to natural hazards than are industrialized countries because of lack of understanding, education, infrastructure, poor building codes. Poverty is in a way directly related to vulnerability of natural hazards - since poverty leads to poor building structure, increased population density, and lack of communication and infrastructure

Human intervention in natural processes increases vulnerability by

1. Development and habitation of lands susceptible to hazards, For example, building on floodplains subject to floods, sea cliffs subject to landslides, coastlines subject to hurricanes and floods, or volcanic slopes subject to volcanic eruptions.

2.Increasing the severity or frequency of a natural hazard. For example: overgrazing or deforestation leading to more severe erosion (floods, landslides), mining groundwater leading to subsidence, construction of roads on unstable slopes leading to landslides.

1.6 Assessing Hazards and Risks

Processes that have been operating since the origin of the Earth produce natural disasters. Such processes are beneficial to us as humans because they are responsible for things that make the Earth a habitable planet for life. For example, throughout the Earth's history, volcanism has been responsible for producing the hydrosphere and the atmosphere. Earthquakes are one of the processes responsible for the formation of mountain ranges, which influences climate zones on the Earth's surface. Erosional processes, including flooding, landslides, and windstorms, replenish soil and helps sustain life. These processes are only considered hazardous when they adversely affect humans and their activities.

a) Hazard Assessment consists of answering the following questions.

- When have hazardous processes occurred in the past?
- Where have hazardous process occurred in the past?
  - ⇛The magnitude and frequency of the past hazardous processes
  - ⇛The likely effects of a process of a given magnitude if it were to occur now.
  - ⇛Making all this information available in a form easily understandable to public officials responsible for making decisions in event of a disaster.

b) Risk Assessment involves not only the assessment of hazards from a scientific point of view, but also the socio-economic impacts of a hazardous event. Risk is a statement of probability that an event will cause a certain amount of damage, or a statement of the economic impact in monetary terms that an event will cause. Risk assessment involves

- ⇛Hazard assessment
- ⇛Location of buildings, highways, and other infrastructure in the areas subject to hazards
- ⇛Potential exposure to the physical effects of a hazardous situation

Risk assessment helps decision makers and scientists to compare and evaluate potential hazards, decide on priorities on what kinds of mitigation are possible, and on where to focus resources.

1.7 Hazard Predictions and Warning

Risk and vulnerability can sometimes be reduced if there is an adequate means of predicting a hazardous event.

a) Prediction

This is the probability that an event will occur based on scientific observations and inferences. It involves monitoring of the process in order to identify some kind of precursor event that may be known to lead to a more hazardous one. For example, volcanic eruptions are usually preceded by a sudden increase in the number of earthquakes immediately below the volcano and changes in the chemical composition of the gases emitted from a volcanic vent. If closely monitored, volcanic eruptions can be often predicted with reasonable accuracy.

b) Forecasting

In the prediction of floods, hurricanes, and other weather related phenomena the word forecast refers to short-term prediction in terms of the magnitude, location, date, and time of an event. For example, weather forecasts, which we regularly see in the television and read in the newspapers. In the prediction of earthquakes, the word forecast is used in a much less precise way – eferring to a long-term probability that is not specific in terms of the exact time that the event will occur. For example, prior to the October 17th, 1989, Loma Prieta Earthquake the U.S. Geological Survey had forecast a 50% probability that a large earthquake would occur in this area within the next 30 years. Even after the event, the current forecast is for a 67% probability that a major earthquake will occur in this area in the next 30 years.

c) Early Warning

A warning is a statement that a high probability of a hazardous event will occur, based on a prediction or forecast. The effectiveness of a warning depends on: the timeliness of the warning, public information systems to inform the general public of the predicted danger and the credibility of the warning authorities.

1.8 Role of Different Individuals

Everyone has a responsibility to understand the effects of a natural hazard and respond to assessments, predictions, and warnings. Education is one of the most important aspects of disaster management and planning.

a) Responsibilities of Scientists and Engineers

Scientists have the expertise to determine where natural hazards exist, and the effects of such hazards when an event occurs and have access to monitoring of processes that enable prediction. Scientists and engineers should make information available to public officials about ways to reduce vulnerability and risk, by suggesting zoning regulations and building codes to public officials. They should help develop early warning systems to effectively communicate such warnings to Public Officials responsible for communicating the warning to the general public. Scientists must also synthesize the information available in form without scientific jargon, which is understandable to all concerned.

b) Responsibilities of public officials and citizens

Public Officials need to be educated about hazard assessments and decide where and how resources are to be allocated to minimize risk. They can help reduce vulnerability by making planning decisions and suggesting proper building codes. Their main responsibility is to inform the public about imminent dangers based on predictions and warnings issued by scientific community. Public officials have to develop plans for evacuation, emergency response, rescue, and recovery. Public officials must be able to communicate effectively with scientific community and the general public to disseminate information.

The citizens need to be aware of the effects of natural hazards on their communities and should have some understanding of what might occur in the event of a disaster. The general public should be informed and prepared about what their response should be when a warning is issued. Citizens can communicate with public officials to help them carry out their responsibilities for hazard and risk reduction.

c) The Role of Teachers and Educators

Teachers and educators have a major role in educating the younger generation about natural hazardous processes and making them aware of possible responses when the disaster strikes. Teachers and educators should have some training in providing first aid treatment, following a disaster, if professional medical assistance is not readily or immediately available. Routine exercises should be held in schools, colleges and universities to provide first aid training to all staff or even to the students themselves.

Natural disasters: international attention and strategies

The decade 1990's was designated as the International Decade for Natural Disaster Reduction (IDNDR) by the United Nations with primary goal to reduce the loss of life, property, socio-economic disruption caused by natural disasters, such as earthquakes, tsunamis, floods, landslides, volcanic eruptions, droughts, locust infestations, and other disasters of natural origin. A strictly techno-centric and scientific approach in the beginning was followed by the IDNDR, but the Yokohama conference in 1994 put socio-economic aspects as component of effective disaster prevention into perspective. A global strategy aiming at reducing the impacts of natural hazards, therefore, must include the development of national and sub-national mechanisms for disaster risk reduction. Within this context the IDNDR advised the UN-member states to establish National Platforms that would facilitate the adjustment of general disaster risk reduction objectives to national/local conditions implement the agreed policies and expand the understanding and perception of the importance of disaster risk reduction on national levels. In practice, there remains a pressing need to revitalize and strengthen these national structures, as many countries have not established national network. The same resolution also designated the second Wednesday of October as International Day for Natural Disaster Reduction. The (international strategy for disaster reduction) ISDR aims to push the initiatives and cooperation agreed on during the IDNDR, and developing new mechanisms as well as ensuring for further commitments from policy-makers. The ultimate goal is to reduce human, social, economic and environmental losses due to natural hazards. The ISDR promotes the following four objectives as tools towards reaching disaster reduction for all:

⇛Increase public awareness to understand risk, vulnerability and disaster reduction globally

⇛Obtain commitment from public authorities to implement disaster reduction policies and actions.

⇛Stimulate interdisciplinary and inter-sectoral partnerships, including the expansion of risk reduction networks.

⇛Improve scientific knowledge about disaster reduction.

In conclusion, hazards are an integral part of life and no one can live in an environment totally risk free. Each hazard varies in dimensions and assessing hazards and risks is the first important step and the response to different hazards requires adopting different strategies.

Natural Service Functions of Natural Hazards:

Natural earth processes are considered only hazardous when they affect human life and property. These earth processes have important service functions, as they are responsible for things that make the Earth a habitable planet for life. Volcanic activity throughout the history of the earth has been responsible for producing the hydrosphere and the atmosphere. Flooding, landslides, and windstorms replenish soil, which sustain life.

When natural calamity occurs:

⇛Do not panic.

⇛Do not spread rumours.

⇛Encourage people to face the situation.

⇛Help people and contribute clothes, food, medicines and cash to agencies involved in rescue operations.

Questions

1. What are the different types of hazards?
2. Write short notes on effects of hazards.
3. Can some natural hazards be predicted with a fair degree of accuracy? Discuss.

Some interesting facts

- The deadliest recorded earthquake occurred in 1557 in central China where an estimated 830,000 people were killed.
- A 1960 Chilean earthquake, which occurred off the coast, had a magnitude of 9.6 and broke a fault more than 1,000 miles long.
- The 1994 Northridge earthquake, which had a magnitude of 6.7, was responsible for approximately 60 deaths, 9,000 injuries, and about $40 billion in damage.
- The Kobe earthquake of 1995 had a magnitude 6.8 and killed 5,530 people. There were some 37,000 injuries and more than $100 billion in economic loss.
- Alaska is one country that experiences a magnitude 7 earthquake almost every year, and a magnitude 8 or greater earthquake on average every 14 years.
- Florida and North Dakota get the fewest earthquakes in the United States of America, even fewer than New York.
- Arica, in Chile, gets just 0.03 inches rain per year and at that rate, it would take about a century to fill a coffee cup.
- Intense rainfall over a short period of time can trigger shallow, fast-moving mud and debris flows. Slow and steady rainfall over a long period of time may trigger deeper, slow-moving landslides.
- Debris flows are like mud avalanches, which can move at speeds more than 100 mph.
- About 540 volcanoes on land are known but there is no record of how many undersea volcanoes have erupted through history.
- In the last 500 years, at least 300,000 people were killed by volcanic activity. Between 1980 and 1990, volcanic activities have killed at least 26,000 people.

• The most prominent topographic feature on Earth is the immense volcanic mountain chain that encircles the planet beneath the sea -- the chain is more than 30,000 miles long and rises an average of 18,000 feet above the seafloor. This is the mid-ocean ridge and where Earth's tectonic plates spread apart as new crust gets formed due to volcanic activity. There are more volcanoes here than on land.

• Most earthquakes are triggered less than 50 miles from the Earth's surface. Shallower earthquakes have more damage potential, but damages due to earthquake depends largely on rock and soil conditions as well as building materials.

• During the volcanic activity on May 18, 1980, Mount St. Helens erupted more than 540 million tons of ash over an area of more than 22,000 square miles. It was the most destructive volcanic eruption known to have occurred in the United States. Estimated $1 billion damage was caused by the eruption, through mudflows and landslides as well as what fell from the sky.

• Astronomers predict that over the next few billion years, thc Sun will swell so large as to envelop our planet Earth. There is a probability, however, that the changing mass of the Sun will cause Earth to move into a more distant and pleasant orbit.

Unit 2

EARTHQUAKES

"We learn geology the morning after the earthquake, on ghastly diagrams of cloven mountains, up heaved plains, and the dry bed of the sea".

Ralph Waldo Emerson (1803–1882),
U.S. essayist, poet, philosopher

Earthquakes provide us the ideal natural laboratory conditions to study the seismic waves generated by them, which reveals about the interior structure of the Earth. A devastating earthquake only confirms that our planet is a dynamic, changing system. Earthquakes are certainly a geologic hazard for those living near the earthquake-prone areas but an earthquake located in remote areas from human population, rarely causes any damage or deaths and does not make news. Earthquake hazard risk depends on the population density, construction standards and of course, emergency preparedness. The risk that an earthquake occurs depends on whether or not tectonic activity that causes deformation is occurring within the crust of that area. An earthquake effect can be understood when compared to the effects observed when a stone is thrown into water. After the stone hits the water a series of concentric waves will move outwards from the centre. The same nature of events occurs in an earthquake. There is a sudden movement within the crust or mantle and concentric shock waves move out from that point.

Plate motions are slow, but they are not always so on a shorter timescale. When the strength of the lithosphere fails suddenly in response to built-up stress, the result is an earthquake. Earthquakes occur when energy stored in elastically strained rocks is suddenly released. This release of energy causes intense ground shaking in the area near the source of the earthquake and sends waves of elastic energy, called seismic waves, throughout the Earth. They occur along faults, planar breaks in rocks along which there is displacement of rocks on one side relative to the other, and they happen when that displacement occurs suddenly in response to stress. Volcanic eruptions can also cause earthquakes.

2.1 Seismic Waves

When an earthquake occurs, the elastic energy is released sending out vibrations, called seismic waves, that travel throughout the Earth. The study of the seismic waves in the Earth is called seismology. The Seismic waves travel through the Earth as vibrations and the instrument used to record these vibrations is called seismometer and the resulting graph that shows the vibrations is called a seismogram. The seismometer must be able to move with the vibrations, yet part of it must remain nearly stationary.

The source of an earthquake is called the focus, which is an exact location within the Earth where seismic waves are generated by sudden release of stored elastic energy, whereas the epicentre is the point on the surface of the Earth directly above the focus (Figure 2.1).

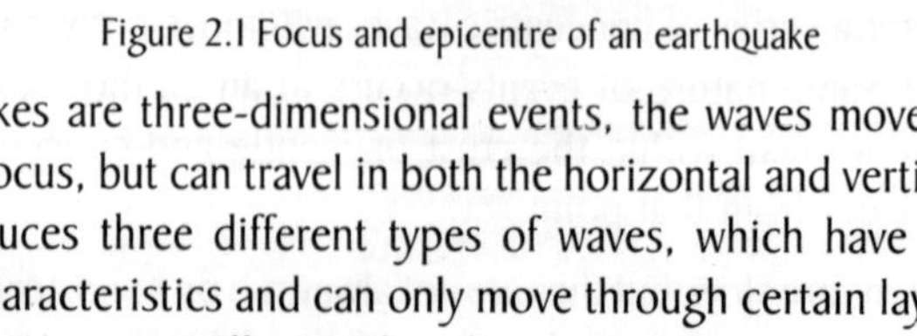

Figure 2.1 Focus and epicentre of an earthquake

Earthquakes are three-dimensional events, the waves move outwards from the focus, but can travel in both the horizontal and vertical plains. This produces three different types of waves, which have their own distinct characteristics and can only move through certain layers within the Earth. Waves travelling within the earth are known as body waves and are of two types: primary (P) and secondary waves (S). The P waves are also called compressional waves and are faster of the two and can travel through solid, liquid and gaseous material. The S waves are called as shear waves and can travel only through solid materials. Waves travelling along the surface of the earth are called surface waves, which cause much damage to buildings and other structures. Surface waves include Love waves that have a complex horizontal ground movement and Rayleigh waves, which have a complex rolling motion. Both travel slower than do the body waves.

Earthquake magnitude – The magnitude of the earthquake is measured by the amount of ground shaking. The size of an earthquake is usually given in terms of a scale called the Richter Magnitude, named after the geophysicist Professor Charles Richter. The Richter Magnitude involves measuring the amplitude of the largest recorded wave at a specific distance from the earthquake.

It usually takes more than one seismographic station to calculate the magnitude of an earthquake. Thus, the media reports the initial estimates of earthquake magnitude immediately after an earthquake and a final assigned magnitude for the same earthquake that may differ from initial estimates, but is assigned after seismologists have had time to evaluate the data from numerous seismographic stations.

2.2 Genesis of Earthquakes

Figure 2.2 Position of rocks before and after release of elastic strain

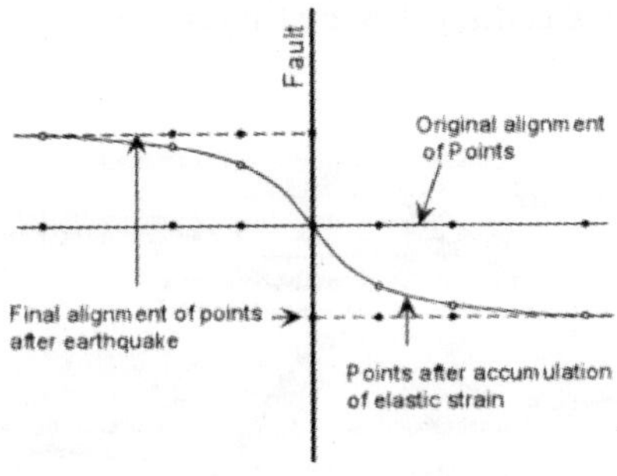

Most natural earthquakes are caused by sudden slippage along a fault zone. This observation was made by making measurements at a

number of points across a fault. The elastic rebound theory suggests that if slippage along a fault is hindered such that elastic strain energy builds up in the deforming rocks on either side of the fault, when the slippage does occur, the energy released causes an earthquake. Prior to an earthquake it was noted that the rocks adjacent to the fault were bending (Figure 2.2). These bends disappeared after an earthquake suggesting that the energy stored in bending the rocks was suddenly released during the earthquake.

2.3 Types of Earthquakes

Earthquakes are almost always classified based on their origin. Therefore, they are most often referred to as tectonic hazards as they originate due to the movements of the plates of the earth's crust known as tectonic activity. Mini earthquakes can be caused by other ways, for example by volcanic activity or by human activity. If volcanic activity is the cause then the earthquake is still classified as a tectonic hazard, as volcanic activities are also tectonic phenomena. Humans can induce earthquakes through a variety of activities, such as the filling of new reservoirs / dams, the underground detonation of atomic explosives, or the pumping of fluids deep into the Earth through wells.

1. Tectonic Earthquakes

Plate tectonics theory explains that the crustal layer of the Earth is made of several plates and how the large areas of crust that floats on the Mantle. Tectonic earthquakes are triggered when the crust becomes

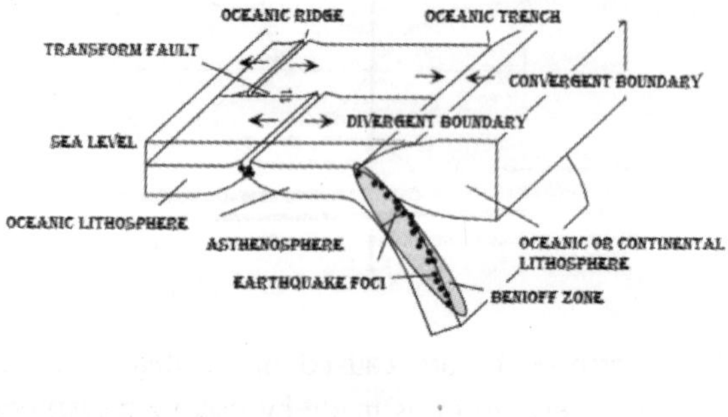

Figure 2.3 Relationship between plate tectonic and earthquakes

subjected to strain, and eventually moves. Since the tectonic plates are free to slowly move, they can either drift towards each other (convergent boundaries), away from each other (divergent boundaries) or slide past each other (transform faults) (Figure 2.3). Benioff zone is a deep active seismic area in a subduction zone and develop beneath volcanic island arcs and continental margins above active subduction zones. Differential motion along the zone produces deep-seated earthquakes, the foci of which may be as deep as about 700 kilometres.

2. Volcanic Earthquakes

Explosive eruption of a volcano can cause volcanic earthquakes. Not all volcanoes are prone to violent eruption, and most are 'quiet' for the majority of the time. When a volcano explodes, it is likely that the associated earthquake effects will be confined to an area 10 to 20 miles around its base, unlike a tectonic earthquake, which may be felt around the globe. The volcanoes which are most likely to explode violently are those which produce acidic lava.

2.4 Distribution of Earthquakes

Earthquake distribution is called seismicity and is highest along relatively narrow belts that coincide with plate boundaries (Figure 2.4). This makes sense, since plate boundaries are zones along which lithospheric plates mover relative to one another. Earthquakes along these zones are either shallow focus earthquakes (that have focal depths less that about 70 km) or deep focus earthquakes (that have focal depths between 75 and 700 km).

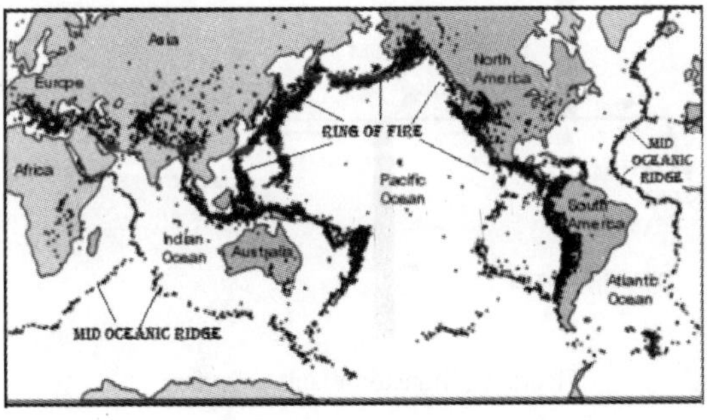

Figure 2.4 World Distributions of Earthquakes

1. Earthquakes at diverging plate boundaries

Diverging plate boundaries are zones where two plates move away from each other, such as at the oceanic ridges. In divergent zones, the lithosphere is in a state of tensional stress and thus normal faults and rift valleys occur. Earthquakes that occur along such boundaries show normal fault motion and tend to be shallow focus earthquakes (with focal depths less than about 20 km). Such shallow focal depths indicate that the brittle lithosphere must be relatively thin along these diverging plate boundaries (Figure 2.5).

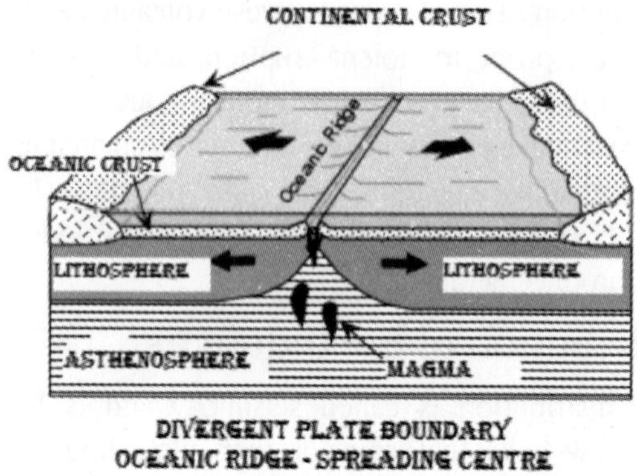

Figure 2.5 Divergent plate boundary

2. Earthquakes at transform plate boundaries

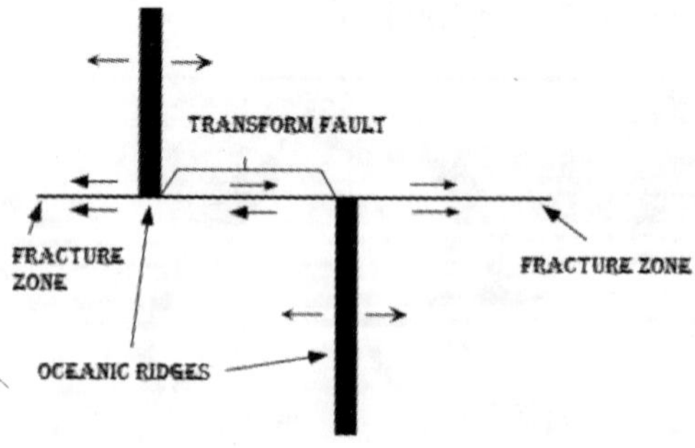

Figure 2.6 Transform fault boundary

Transform fault boundaries are plate boundaries where lithospheric plates slide past one another in a horizontal fashion. Earthquakes along these boundaries show strike-slip motion on the faults and tend to be shallow focus earthquakes (with depths usually less than about 50 km). For example, the San Andreas Fault of California (Figure 2.6).

3. Earthquakes at converging plate boundaries

Convergent plate boundaries are boundaries where two plates run into each other and compressional stresses are active and thus reverse faults or thrust faults are common. There are two types of converging plate boundaries. (1) Subduction boundaries, where oceanic lithosphere is pushed beneath either oceanic or continental lithosphere and (2) collision boundaries where two plates with continental lithosphere collide (Figure 2.7).

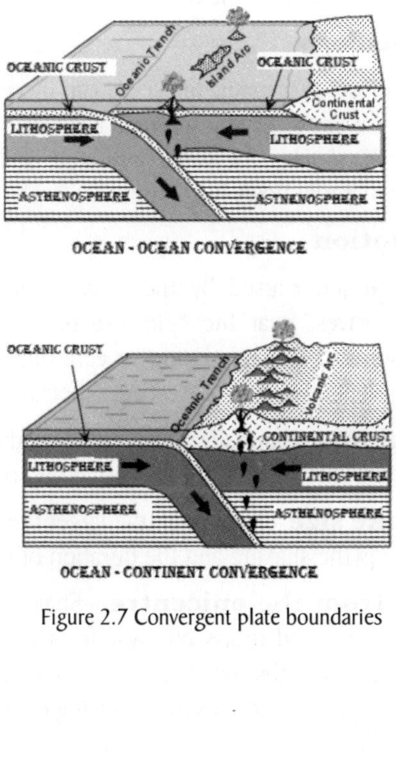

Figure 2.7 Convergent plate boundaries

2.5 Earthquake Hazards

Earthquakes can damage the infrastructure. For example, roads and bridges can be impassable, water pressure can fail, and gas lines can break and leak. As a result, fires can spread unchecked and often do much of the damage in earthquakes.

1. Damage to Buildings

The three main characteristics of the seismic waves affecting the potential for building damage experienced during an earthquake are:

- The amplitude of the waves (depends on earthquake size and distance from the event).
- The duration of shaking (which increases for larger earthquakes).
- The frequency content of the waves.

2. Surface Geology

The soil/rock type, water content, thickness can increase or decrease the amplitude of the shaking. One particular hazard is liquefaction, which occurs when shaking of water-saturated soils changes the behaviour and the material flows like a fluid.

3. Ground Motion

Shaking of the ground caused by the passage of seismic waves, especially surface waves, near the epicentre of the earthquake are responsible for the most damage during an earthquake. The intensity of ground shaking depends on the following aspects:

- **Local geology** - Generally, loose unconsolidated sediment is subject to more intense shaking than solid bedrock.
- **Earthquake size** - In general, the larger the earthquake, the more intense is the shaking and the duration of the shaking.
- **Distance from the epicentre** - Shaking is most severe near the epicentre and drops off away from the epicentre. The distance factor depends on the type of material underlying the area. Damage to structures from shaking depends on the type of construction.

4. Fault zone

Ground rupture generally occurs only along the fault zone that moves during the earthquake. Thus, structures that are built across fault zones may collapse, whereas structures built adjacent to, but not crossing the fault, may survive.

5. Aftershocks

Aftershocks occur because the main earthquake changes the stress pattern in areas around the epicentre, and the crust must adjust to these changes. These are usually smaller earthquakes that occur after a main earthquake (1260 aftershocks were measured after the 1964 Alaskan Earthquake). Aftershocks are generally very dangerous because they cause further collapse of structures already damaged by the main shock.

6. Other Secondary Hazards related to Earthquakes

• **Mass movements** - In mountainous regions and hilly terrains subjected to earthquakes, ground shaking may trigger landslides, rock and debris falls, rock and debris slides, slumps, and debris avalanches.

• **Flooding** - Flooding can be a secondary effect that may occur due to rupture of human made dams, due to tsunamis, and as a result of ground subsidence after an earthquake.

• **Fire** - Fire is a secondary effect of earthquakes. Because power lines and natural gas lines may rupture due to an earthquake, fires are often started closely following an earthquake.

• **Contamination of water** – Earthquakes can cause ground water contamination and serious health hazards.

• **Liquefaction** - Liquefaction is a process that occurs in water-saturated unconsolidated sediment due to shaking. In areas underlain by such material, the ground shaking causes the grains to lose grain to grain contact, and thus the material tends to flow.

• **Changes in Ground Level** - Earthquakes may cause both uplift and subsidence of the land surface, a secondary or tertiary effect that is caused by faulting. During the 1964 Alaskan Earthquake, some areas were uplifted up to 11.5 meters, while other areas subsided up to 2.3 meters.

2.6 Predictions and Control of Earthquakes

On the basis of geologic knowledge, we can predict that most earthquakes will occur along the plate boundaries. We can also predict the average rate of occurrence (over millions of years). Such predictions are not of practical use for society given the time frame of prediction, although they are not without value since they improve our understanding of the basic processes of earthquakes. However, although predicting the exact time of an earthquake would be valuable, it does not solve all of our problems. The best preparation for earthquakes is appropriate building construction. The information geoscientists try to provide is the level of shaking expected in a given region by mapping the surface geology, the potential size and location of earthquakes.

1. Long-Term Forecasting

Knowledge of present tectonic setting, historical records, and geological records are studied to determine locations and recurrence intervals of earthquakes. Long-term forecasting is based mainly on the knowledge of when and where earthquakes have occurred in the past. Two aspects of this study are important, the study of prehistoric earthquakes, i.e. Paleoseismology and Seismic gaps. A seismic gap is a zone along a tectonically active area where no earthquakes have occurred recently, but it is known that elastic strain is building in the rocks. If a seismic gap can be identified, then it might be an area expected to have a large earthquake in the near future.

2. Short-Term Prediction

Despite the availability of numerous possible precursor events that are possible to monitor, successful short-term earthquake prediction has so far been very difficult. Short-term predication involves monitoring of processes that occur in the vicinity of earthquake-prone faults for activity that signify a pending earthquake. Anomalous events or processes that may precede an earthquake are called precursor events and might signal a coming earthquake. Among the precursor events that may be important are the following:

- **Uplift of ground and their tilting**- Measurements taken around active faults sometimes show that prior to an earthquake the ground is uplifted or tilted due to the swelling of rocks caused by strain building on the fault. This may lead to the formation of numerous small cracks. This cracking in the rocks may lead to small earthquakes called foreshocks.

- **Foreshocks** - Prior to a 1975 earthquake in China, the observation of numerous foreshocks led to successful prediction of an earthquake and evacuation of the city of Haicheng. The magnitude 7.3 earthquake that occurred, destroyed half of the city of about 100 million inhabitants, but resulted in only a few hundred deaths because of the successful evacuation.

- **Shift in water level in wells** - As rocks become strained in the vicinity of a fault, changes in pressure of the groundwater (water existing in the pore spaces and fractures in rocks) occur. This may force the groundwater to move to higher or lower elevations, causing changes in the water levels in wells.

- **Emission of Radon gas** – Radon is an inert gas produced by the radioactive decay of uranium and other elements in rocks. Radon, being inert, does not combine with other elements to form compounds, and thus remains in a crystal structure until some event forces it out. Deformation resulting from strain may force the Radon out and lead to emissions of Radon that show up in well water. The newly formed micro cracks could serve as pathways for the Radon to escape into groundwater. Increases in the amount of radon emissions have been reported prior to some earthquakes.

- **Drop in the Electrical Resistivity of Rocks** - In general, rocks are poor conductors of electricity, but water is more efficient in conducting electricity. If micro cracks develop and groundwater is forced into the cracks, this may cause the electrical resistivity to decrease (causing the electrical conductivity to increase-electrical resistivity is the resistance to the flow of electric current). In some cases a 5-10% drop in electrical resistivity has been observed prior to an earthquake.

• **Unusual Radio Waves** - Just prior to the Loma Prieta Earthquake of 1989, some researchers reported observing unusual radio waves. Where these were generated and why, is not yet known, but research is underway.

• **Strange animal behaviour** - Prior to magnitude 7.4 earthquakes in Tanjin, China, zookeepers reported unusual animal behaviour. Snakes refusing to go into their holes, swans refusing to go near water, pandas screaming. This was the first systematic study of this phenomenon prior to an earthquake.

2.7 Controlling Earthquakes

Although no attempts have yet been made to control earthquakes, earthquakes have been known to be induced by human interaction with the Earth, which suggests that in the future earthquake control may be possible. Earthquakes are caused by forces strong enough to move continents and human efforts cannot stop them from occurring. However, moderation of some of their most severe effects may be possible for example by using the fluid- injection technique.

Case Studies of Earthquakes

The Uttarkashi earthquake and its proximity to Tehri dam

The 1991 Uttarkashi earthquake in the Tehri region of the Gharwal Himalaya shook the north-central India, which had a magnitude of 6.5, attracting great attention due to its location near the high Tehri dam. This event killed many people and damaged completely or partially about 48,000 houses and was instrumentally recorded and studied. The earthquake occurred due to slippage along the Main Central Thrust, a major tectonic boundary that divides lesser Himalayan terrain in the south from the snow clad mountains in the north.

Some other examples of earthquakes:

• The worst earthquake in recorded history occurred in 1556 in Shaaxi, China, killing 830,000 people, mostly living in caves, excavated in poorly consolidated loess (wind deposited silt and clay).

• Another earthquake also occurred in China (T'ang Shan Province), killed 240,000 in 1976, with a magnitude of 7.8 on Richter scale. Deaths were due to collapse of masonry (brick) buildings.

• Contrast the above mentioned earthquake events with the following example- In earthquake prone areas like California, in order to reduce earthquake risk, there are strict building codes requiring the design and construction of buildings and other structures that will withstand a large earthquake. While this program is not always completely successful, one fact stands out to prove its effectiveness. In 1989 an earthquake near San Francisco, California (The Loma Prieta, or World Series Earthquake) with a Richter Magnitude of 7.1 killed about 62 people. Most were killed when a double-decked freeway in Oakland collapsed.

• For the sake of comparison, about 10 months later, an earthquake with magnitude 6.9 occurred in Armenia, where no earthquake-proof building codes existed. The death toll in the latter earthquake was about 25,000. It is correctly said that, "Earthquakes don't kill people, but buildings do". This is because buildings or other human construction falling down during an earthquake causes most deaths from earthquakes.

Human induced earthquakes

• For ten years after construction of the Hoover Dam, in Nevada, blocking the Colorado River to produce Lake Mead, over 600 earthquakes occurred, one with magnitude of 5.2 and another with a magnitude of 4.

• In the late 1960s, toxic waste injected into hazardous waste disposal wells at Rocky Flats, near Denver apparently caused earthquakes to occur in a previously considered earthquake safe area. The focal depths of the quakes ranged between 4 and 8 km, just below the 3.8

km-deep wells. In the above examples, the increased seismicity was apparently due to increasing fluid pressure in the rocks, which resulted in re-activating older faults, by increasing strain.

•Nuclear testing in Nevada set off thousands of aftershocks after the explosion of a 6.3 magnitude equivalent underground nuclear test. The largest aftershocks were about magnitude 5.

Natural Service functions of earthquakes:

Earthquake can bring to the surface of the earth valuable resources, which otherwise can remain out of reach deep inside the earth. They tell us about the internal structure of the earth.

When an earthquake occurs

Before

⇛Always have fire extinguishers, keep first-aid kits at home and learn about their usage.

⇛Heavy objects should not be kept on shelves as they fall during earthquakes and heavy furniture, cupboards, and appliances should be anchored to the walls.

During

⇛Stay calm and if caught indoors, stand against a wall near the centre of the building, stand in a doorway, or crawl under heavy furniture like a table. Stay away from windows and doors.

⇛If outdoors, stay in the open away from power lines or any object that might fall and stay away from buildings that can fall.

⇛If in a car, stop the car and stay inside the car until the earthquake stops.

After

⇛Check yourself and others for injuries. Provide first aid for anyone who needs it.

⇛Check water, gas, power and electric lines for damage. If any are damaged, shut off the valves.

⇛Listen to the radio, television.

⇛Stay away from damaged buildings.

⇛Wear boots or sturdy shoes, as there may be broken glass, debris, etc.

⇛Be aware of aftershocks, which may strike after an earthquake has occurred.

2.8 Tsunami

Tsunami is a series of huge waves that occur after an undersea disturbance, such as an earthquake or volcano eruption. Tsunami gets its name from the Japanese word for harbour wave. The waves travel in all directions from the area of disturbance, just like the ripples that happen after throwing a rock. The waves may travel in the open sea and can be as fast as 450 miles per hour. As the big waves approach shallow waters along the coast they grow to a great height and smash into the shore. They can be as high as about 100 feet. They can cause a lot of destruction on the shore. Though they have nothing to do with tides, they are sometimes mistakenly called tidal waves.

Tsunamis can also travel across oceans, so a large earthquake along the coast of South America can produce a tsunami that eventually damages coastal regions of Hawaii and Japan. They travel about as fast as an aeroplane, so there is sufficient time to warn distant localities. But they can strike within a few minutes close to the earthquake. The speed of this wave depends on the ocean depth and is typically about 712 km/hr. This is relatively slow compared to seismic waves, so we are often informed and alerted to the dangers of the tsunami by the shaking before the wave arrives. These waves are typically more devastating to the coastal region than the shaking of the earthquake that caused the tsunami. Even the more common tsunamis of about 10-20 meters can totally devastate coastal communities. Strong and devastating tsunamis occur once in every one to two years and they have at times killed thousands of people. In 1992-93 three large tsunamis occurred: Japan, Indonesia, and Nicaragua. All struck at night and devastated the local communities.

2.9 Hazards Associated with Tsunamis

The primary damage from tsunami comes basically from the destructive nature of the waves themselves. Secondary effects include the debris which can act as projectiles which they run into other objects, erosion that can undermine the foundations of structures built along coastlines, and fires that result from disruption of gas and electrical lines. Tertiary effects include loss of crops and water that can lead to famine and disease.

2.10 Tsunami Prediction and Early Warning Systems

For areas located at great distances from earthquakes that could potentially generate a tsunami there is usually plenty of time for warnings to be sent and coastal areas evacuated, even though tsunami travel at high velocities across the oceans. Hawaii is a good example of an area located far from most of the sources of tsunami, where early warning is possible and has saved lives. For earthquakes occurring anywhere on the subduction margins of the Pacific Ocean there is a minimum of 4 hours of warning before a tsunami would strike any of the Hawaiian Islands.

The National Oceanic and Atmospheric Administration (NOAA) have set up a Pacific warning system for areas in the Pacific Ocean, called the Pacific Tsunami Warning Centre. It consists of an international network of seismographic stations, and tidal stations around the Pacific basin that can all send information via satellite to the Centre located in Hawaii. When an earthquake occurs somewhere in the region, the Centre immediately begins to analyse the data looking for signs that the earthquake could have generated a tsunami. The tidal stations are also monitored, and if a tsunami is detected, a warning is sent out to all areas on the Pacific coast.

In conclusion, to minimize the hazards from Tsunami will require installing of warning systems and to minimize hazards from earthquakes will require further research about the hazard and engineering solutions that reduce vulnerability to ground motion resulting from earthquakes.

Some Case Studies Of Tsunami

The 1946 Scotch Point Light station Tsunami

On April 1, 1946, about 150 km south of Unimak Island in the Aleutians, a large earthquake offset the ocean floor and rattled a light station operated by U. S. Coast Guard personnel. Unknown to the light station operators, the earthquake had also generated a large tsunami. It took about 50 minutes for the waves to travel across the shallow continental shelf and arrive at the light station. The weather was clear and calm and the five-story light station was about 32 feet above sea-level. The crew heard a large roar from the sea just before a 100-foot high tsunami struck and completely demolished the station, killing all inside.

The killer Indian Ocean Tsunami in 2004

On the morning of December 26, 2004, an earthquake of magnitude 9.1 occurred along the oceanic trench off the coast of Sumatra in Indonesia. This large earthquake resulted in vertical displacement of the sea floor and generated a tsunami that eventually killed 280,000 people and affected the lives of several million people. The earthquake released stored elastic energy of approximately 23,000 Hiroshima atomic bombs and uplifted seafloor several meters, displacing billions of gallons of seawater. It set off massive waves (tsunami) that raced out toward the west and east and over a period of 10 hours, the tsunami struck coasts of over 12 countries. The major damage and deaths were around Indian Ocean from SE Asia to East Africa. Although people living on the coastline near the epicentre of the earthquake had little time or warning of the approaching tsunami, those living farther away along the coasts of Thailand, Sri Lanka, India and East Africa had plenty of time to move higher ground to escape. It was one of the most devastating natural disasters in modern human history where 1,50,000 people were killed directly by earthquake and tsunami, millions injured, of which one-third of dead are children (also left tens of thousands of orphans), over 5 million homeless and without basic needs (water, food, shelter). The World had mobilized one of the greatest disaster relief efforts in history. There was no tsunami warning system in place in the

Indian Ocean, and although other tsunami warning centres attempted to provide a warning, there was no effective communication system in place. Unfortunately, it has taken a disaster of great magnitude to point out the failings of the world's scientific community and to educate almost every person on the planet about tsunami.

Natural Service functions of Tsunami:

There are very few benefits of tsunami but it may bring nutrients and sediments needed by soil.

When Tsunami occurs

Before and during

⇛Be connected to radio, television, Internet for tsunami warnings if an earthquake occurs.

⇛In case of a tsunami move inland to higher ground immediately and stay there.

⇛Always stay away from the beach and coastal areas.

After

⇛Stay away from flooded and damaged areas until official advice.

⇛Stay away from debris in water as it can cause hazards.

Questions

1. What is an earthquake and explain the different types based on their origin?
2. Discuss the distribution of earthquakes.
3. What are the hazards associated with earthquakes?
4. Discuss the short and long-term prediction of earthquakes.
5. What is a tsunami and discuss the advantages of installing warning systems?

Some interesting facts

- Thousands of earthquakes occur on the earth daily, though most of them are too weak to be felt.
- Approximately 10,000 people, on an average, die as a result of earthquakes every year.
- The Himalayan frontal arc is one of the seismically active regions of the world.
- The Himalayan collision zone is marked by intense seismic activity and four great earthquake events have (1897 Assam, 1905 Kangra; 1934 Bihar-Nepal and 1950 Assam) occurred in this region in a short span of 53 years.
- An Alaskan earthquake in 1964 generated a tsunami with waves between 10 and 20 feet high along parts of the California, Oregon and Washington coasts.
- In 1946, a tsunami with waves of 20 to 32 feet crashed into Hilo, Hawaii, flooding the downtown area.
- Hawaii is one of the states at greatest risk for a tsunami. They get around one a year, with a damaging tsunami happening about every seven years. California, Oregon and Washington experience a damaging tsunami about every 18 years.
- Long before the modern electronic recordings of earthquakes, scientists built large spring-pendulum seismometers to record the long-period motion produced by such quakes. The largest spring-pendulum seismometers weighed about 15 tons and there is a medium-sized one, three stories high, in Mexico City that is still in operation. The first such "pendulum seismoscope" to measure the shaking of the ground during an earthquake was developed in 1751.
- The average rate of motion across the San Andreas Fault Zone during the past 3 million years is 2 in/yr, which is the same rate at which our fingernails grow. At this rate scientists predict that Los Angeles and San Francisco will be adjacent to one another in approximately 15 million years.

• Moonquakes which are like earthquakes occur on the moon but they occur even less frequently and have smaller magnitudes as compared with those on the Earth. It appears they could be related to the tidal stresses associated with the varying distance between the Earth and Moon.

• The world's greatest land mountain range is the Himalaya-Karakoram. It contains 96 of the world's 109 peaks of over 24,000 ft. The longest range is the Andes of South America which is 7564 km in length and both were created by the movement of tectonic plates.

• Aristotle, the Greek scientist, recognized as early as 350 BC that soft ground shakes more than hard rock in an earthquake.

• British engineer, John Michell, one of the first fathers of seismology, stated the cause of earthquakes correctly in 1760, in a memoir that earthquakes originates due to "shifting masses of rock miles below the surface".

• The interior of Antarctica is reported to have ice quakes which are much smaller but more frequent than earthquakes in Antarctica. The ice quakes are similar to earthquakes, but occur within the ice sheet itself instead of the land underneath the ice.

Unit3

VOLCANOES

"Volcanoes are one way Earth gives birth to itself."

Robert Gross

Volcanoes spew out magma and gases, which result in adding rock material, atmosphere and hydrosphere. Volcanic activity only confirms that our planet is dynamic and constantly changing. Natural processes bring about a change and alter the surface structures and landscape features. Most of the changes are gradual and are hardly noticed. Some changes are rapid and have an important impact on people and their daily lives. Beneath the surface of the earth, changes are occurring as well. Once again, most of the changes are gradual and go unnoticed. Some of them, however, are very sudden and can change our lives. Volcanic eruptions bring molten rock material from inside the earth to the surface. Volcanoes are openings in the surface of the earth from which molten rock, magma and gases escape, which consists of a fissure in the earth's crust above, which a cone of volcanic material has, accumulates. At the top of the cone, is a bowl-shaped vent called a crater. The cone is formed by the deposition of molten or solid material that flows or is ejected through the vent from the interior of the earth.

Most volcanoes are dormant and there are around 600 active volcanoes. Volcanoes may erupt in a quiet manner by spewing fountains of lava high into the air without an explosion or violence. Some volcanoes alternate between quiet and explosive, i.e., Stromboli, near Sicily. Active volcanoes are those that have recently erupted or those that are in the process of erupting, such as Mt. Helens in the state of Washington. Dormant volcanoes still show signs of some activity but have not erupted for some time. Extinct volcanoes show no signs of activity and have not erupted for long periods of time.

3.1 Distribution of Volcanoes

Plate tectonic theory tells us that volcanoes and earthquakes are not randomly distributed around the globe; rather they tend to be concentrated along limited zones or belts along plate boundaries (See Figure 2.4). According to the theory of plate tectonics, the Earth's outer shell (lithosphere) is made up of seven large and many smaller moving plates. When the plates move, their boundaries collide, spread apart or slide past one another, resulting in geological processes such as earthquakes, volcanoes and mountain making. Some volcanoes (like in the Hawaiian Islands) occur in the middle of plates in areas known as hot spots, which is the location above a hot upwelling plume of mantle.

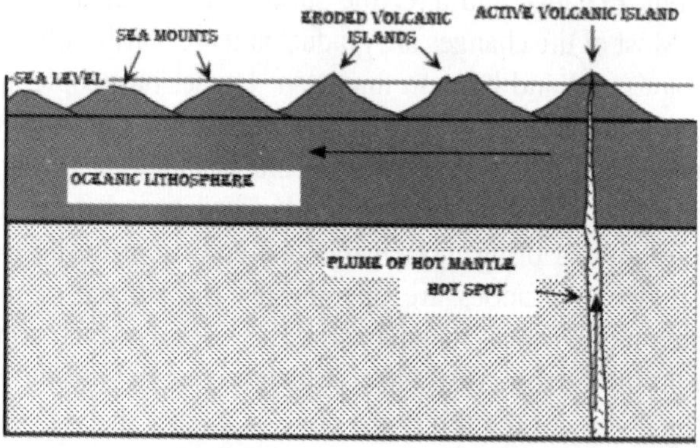

Figure 3.1 Hotspot and volcanoes

Volcanoes normally occur around certain places of the earth's crust. They occur in the following areas:

- Along subduction boundaries at continental plate-oceanic plate convergence (Mt Saint Helens or oceanic plate – oceanic plate convergence (Japan and Philippines)
- Ring of Fire surrounding Pacific Ocean.
- Hot spots (Hawaiian Islands mantle plumes) (Figure 3.1)

• Spreading centres mid-ocean ridges (Iceland), rift valleys (Mt. Kilamanjaro, Africa)

3.2 Different Parts of a Volcano

The main parts include the following (Figure 3.2, 3.3):

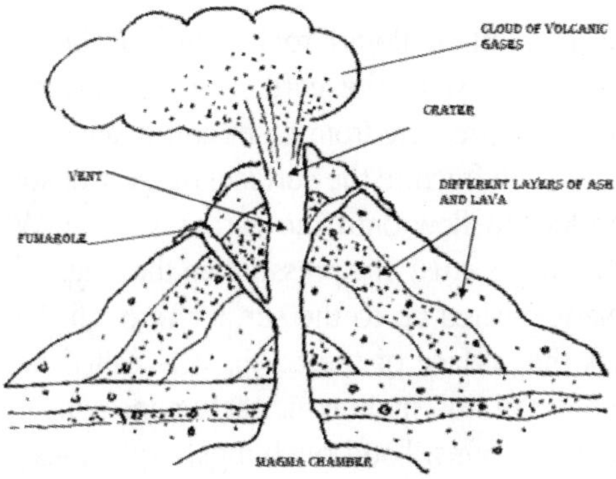

Figure 3.2 Parts of a volcano

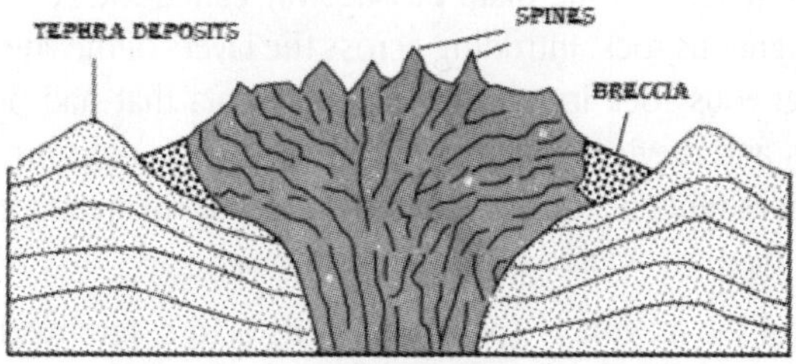

Figure 3.3 Cross Section of a volcanic dome

1. **Crater** – depression at the summit of a volcano, connected by a vent or pipe to the magma chamber below.

2. **Caldera** - crater more than 1 km in diameter, formed at the summit of a volcano when lava is drained from an underground magma chamber, causing the summit of the volcano to be unsupported, and to collapse.

3. **Pit crater** - collapse features on the flanks or summit of a volcano that are smaller than the main caldera at the summit of a volcano.

4. **Vent** - pipe-like conduit connecting the magma chamber to the surface.

5. **Fumaroles** - secondary vents on the flank of a volcano, which emits steam and other gases.

3.3 Volcanic Eruption Process

A large mass of molten, liquid rock, which is under tremendous pressure below the crust of the earth is called magma. A volcanic eruption occurs when pressure from gases and steam within the magma build up sufficiently to fracture the surface, or layer of solid rock above them, allowing lava to flow onto the earth's surface. When fractures occur within the earth's crust, the pressure on the magma becomes less, and the magma is pushed up to the surface through the crack. When magma reaches the surface of the earth, it is called lava. With each successive eruption of hot, molten matter, a cone-shaped mountain or hill of lava gradually forms. Loud rumblings, explosions, steam, gases, rocks, cinders, and ashes may accompany erupting lavas. The opening at the top of a volcano is called the crater. Connecting the crater and the pool of magma is the main passageway called the vent. Dikes are masses of igneous rock, intruding across the layers of the volcanic cone. Sills are igneous rock layers formed by magma that had been forced into cracks and crevices of subsurface rock layers. Volcanic action not only produces igneous rocks but may also help form metamorphic rocks due to the heat associated with the eruptions.

Viscosity of the magma is controlled by its acidic, intermediate or the basic nature. If the lava is acidic (rich in silica) it will harden and set quickly, moving only short distances from its source. It will form the typical volcano shape, a steep-sided cone. Such volcanoes erupt violently because the rapidly hardened rock blocks the vents and allows pressure to build up under the blockage. Such volcanoes are called Composite Volcanoes. Examples are Mount Etna in Sicily, Mount St. Helens in the USA and Mount Vesuvius in Italy. If it is basic lava (low in silica but rich in iron) it flows freely and sets slowly. This allows it to flow long distances from its source, forming layers of gently sloping lava. Such volcanoes are called Shield Volcanoes, and are typical of areas such as Hawaii. Composite, or stratovolcanoes, are typically steep-sided and may be created over many thousands of years - possibly hundreds of thousands of years - and dozens of eruptions. They are slowly built up by the repeated eruption of lava flows, pyroclastic flows and ash, forming a cone shape with steep sides and a crater at the top.

All volcanic eruptions ultimately result in transporting material from the interior of the earth to the surface. The extruded rocks build up mountains, islands, and lava flows, some of which have added to the growth of the continents. The gases and volatiles brought up to the surface have built up the atmosphere and oceans. All of the present atmosphere and oceans have come from the interior. Studying how volatiles come out of the volcanic eruptions today has convinced the scientists that volcanoes have always been the main sources of gas transfer from the interior to the surface. If we take the current rate at which theses gases are emerging, and calculate the cumulative volumes over the history of the planet, we can only account for about 25% of the total water, chlorine, and nitrogen at the surface. This implies that if volcanism has always been the main source of atmospheric gases, there must have been more intensive volcanism, and there could have been larger gas fluxes in the past.

3.4 Kinds of Volcanic Eruptions

Volcanic eruptions, especially explosive ones, are very dynamic phenomena as the behaviour of the eruption is continually changing throughout the duration of the eruption. They can be classified according to the principal types of behaviour that they exhibit namely:

1. Non-explosive Eruptions

Non-explosive eruptions occur due to low gas content and low viscosity magmas (basaltic to andesitic magmas). If the viscosity is low, non-explosive eruptions usually begin with fire fountains due to release of dissolved gases. If the viscosity is high, but the gas content is low, then the lava will pile up over the vent to produce a lava dome or volcanic dome. Lava flows are produced on the surface, and these run like liquids down slope, along the lowest areas they can find. Lava flows produced by eruptions under water are called pillow lavas.

2. Explosive Eruptions

Explosive eruptions occur due to the high gas content and high viscosity magmas (andesitic to rhyolitic magmas). Explosive bursting of bubbles will fragment the magma into clots of liquid that will cool as they fall through the air. These solid particles become pyroclasts and tephra or volcanic ash, which refer to sand-sized or smaller fragments. Blocks are angular fragments that were solid when ejected. Bombs have an aerodynamic shape indicating they were liquid when ejected. Bombs and lapilli's that consist mostly of gas bubbles (vesicles) result in a low-density highly vesicular rock fragment called pumice. Gas clouds and volcanic ash that rise above a volcano produce an eruption column that can rise up to 45 km into the atmosphere. Eventually, the tephra in the eruption column will be acted upon by the wind, carried for some distance, and then fall back to the surface as a tephra fall or ash fall. When the eruption column collapses, a pyroclastic flow will occur, wherein gas and tephra rush down the flanks of the volcano at high speed and is the most dangerous type of volcanic eruption. The deposits that are produced are called ignimbrites if they contain pumice or pyroclastic flow deposits if they contain non-vesicular blocks. If the gas pressure inside the magma is directed outward instead of upward, a lateral blast can occur. When this occurs on the flanks of a lava dome, pyroclastic flows called a glowing avalanche or nuée ardentes (in French) can also result. Directed blasts often result from sudden exposure of the magma by a landslide or collapse of a lava dome.

3.5 Factors Controlling Volcanic Eruptions

Viscosity of the magma controls the type of volcano. Viscosity is controlled by:

1. Magma composition, temperature and viscosity

Viscosity is the resistance to flow and depends primarily on the composition of the magma and temperature. Viscosity is an important property in determining the eruptive behaviour of magmas. Higher silica content magmas (granitic) have higher viscosity than lower silica content magmas (basaltic). Granitic/sialic magma (acidic) is more viscous (stiffer) than basaltic/mafic (basic) magma. Basaltic or mafic magmas tend to be fairly less viscous. Also, hotter lavas are less viscous. The shapes of volcanoes depend on the viscosity of the magma. For example, Basaltic lava will not form a steep cone; but forms relatively flat shield volcanoes. Gases are not easily released from stiff, viscous magmas or lava. Here, the pressure builds up and when the pressure builds high enough, violent explosions occur. These are typical of composite cones or strato-volcanoes.

2. Characteristics of Magma: They control the kind of eruption that would take place.

a) Magma types

Types of magma are determined by the chemical composition of the magma and three broad general types are recognized:

- Basaltic magma -- SiO_2 45-55 wt%, high in Fe, Mg, Ca, low in K, Na
- Andesitic magma --SiO_2 55-65 wt%, intermediate in Fe, Mg, Ca, Na, K
- Rhyolitic magma --SiO_2 65-75%, low in Fe, Mg, Ca, high in K, Na

b) Gases in Magmas

Explosive character of magmas is due to the presence of gases in them as volume of gas expands as pressure is reduced. At depth, in the Earth nearly all magmas contain gas dissolved in the liquid, but the gas forms a separate vapour phase when pressure is decreased as the magma rises toward the surface of the Earth. The composition of the gases in magma is: mostly H_2O (water vapour and some CO_2) and trace amounts of sulphur, chlorine, and fluorine. Rhyolitic magmas (acidic) usually have higher gas contents than basaltic magmas (basic) as the amount of gas present in magma is related to the chemical composition of the magma.

c) Magma temperature

Laboratory measurement and limited field observation indicate that the eruption temperature of various magmas is as follows:

- Basaltic magma - 1000 to 1200°C
- Andesitic magma -800 to 1000°C
- Rhyolitic magma -650 to 800°C.

3.6 Products of Volcanic Eruptions

The products of volcanic eruptions include the following: Lava flows, pyroclastic debris, gases and Nuee ardentes

1. Lava flows

2. Pyroclastic debris, volcanic bombs, ash and dust, lapilli (walnut-sized) and cinders

In addition to the gases that come out of volcanoes, there are large amounts of solid materials ejected; typically the smaller particles of dust reach the highest levels in the atmosphere. For strong vertical eruptions, dust can be propelled up into the stratosphere, above 17 kilometres. There, the suspended dust particles can block solar radiation, effectively by heating up the stratosphere while the lower troposphere cools causing short-term effects.

3. Gases

Volcanic gas samples reveal large amounts of water (H_2O; 70 %), carbon dioxide (CO_2; 15 %) and Nitrogen (N_2 5 %) coming out today, along with smaller amounts of sulphur dioxide (SO_2), Hydrogen sulphide (H_2S), carbon monoxide (CO), Hydrogen (H_2), hydrochloric acid (HCl), and Methane (CH_4), Cl, Ar.

4. Nuee ardentes

They are glowing clouds of volcanic gases (steam) and pyroclastic debris (ash), which avalanche down the side of a volcano. They can reach speeds of about 200 km/hr. A nuee ardente from Mount Pelee, on the Caribbean island of Martinique, destroyed the town of St. Pierre in 1902, killing about 28,000 inhabitants.

3.7 Hazards Associated with Volcanoes

Volcanic hazards are classified into primary and secondary hazards:

- Primary: Lava, Ash, Nuee Ardentes, Gas

• Secondary: Lahars, Tsunami, and Agricultural.

1. Primary volcanic hazards

Lava flows are usually not very dangerous, as they move rather slowly but are damaging to property. But, there are a few exceptions. For example, the 1977 Nyiragongo (Zaire) volcano had a side fissure drain the lava lake in the main crater very rapidly, with lava squirting out at 60 miles per hour. This caused approximately 1000 fatalities.

• **Violent Eruptions and Pyroclastic Activity** - They are the most dangerous as they can travel so rapidly that few humans can escape. Hot pyroclastic flows cause death by suffocation and burning.

• **Ash falls** are typified by the 79 AD eruption of Mt. Vesuvius, which blanketed Pompeii and Herculaneum with mud ash and gas, causing about 20,000 fatalities.

• **Nuee Ardente** is fast moving flows of gas and magma, in a volcanic avalanche. These are very deadly, as they flow fast and with utter destruction. Some examples include the 1902 eruption of La Soufriere, St. Vincent, which killed 1500.

• **Gas emissions** accompany every volcano, which are often poisonous to living organisms, but in some cases there are special conditions that allow the gases to build up. Some of the poisonous gases include: Hydrogen Chloride (HCl), Hydrogen Sulphide (H_2S), Hydrogen Fluoride (HF), and Carbon Dioxide (CO_2). The 1783 eruption of Mt. Laki, Iceland, had a massive flux of sulphuric and fluorine gas, which killed great numbers of livestock. The ensuing famine led to 10,000 fatalities. In 1984, CO_2 gas escaping from the bottom of Lake Monoun, a crater lake in the African country of Cameroon, killed 37 people.

2. Secondary and Tertiary Volcanic hazards

• **Lahars** are volcanic mudflows, typically resulting from eruption under ice and snow at the summit, which mixes with the ash to make fast flowing muds. Agricultural catastrophes are secondary consequences of the widespread devastation of volcanic eruptions. These hazards are varied and clearly not easily controlled.

• **Tephra falls** - Volcanoes can emit huge quantities of loose, unconsolidated tephra, which become deposited on the landscape. They are subject to rapid removal if they are exposed to a source of water. The source of water can be derived by melting of snow or ice during the eruption, emptying of crater lakes during an eruption, or rainfall. They can cause the collapse of roofs and can affect areas far from the eruption. Although tephra falls blanket an area like snow, they are far more destructive because tephra deposits have a density more than twice that of snow and tephra deposits do not melt like snow. Tephra falls destroy vegetation, including crops, and can kill livestock that eat the ash-covered vegetation. Tephra falls can cause loss of agricultural activity for years after an eruption.

• **Debris Avalanches and Debris Flows** - Volcanic Mountains tend to become over steepened due to the addition of new material over time as well due to inflation of the mountain as magma intrudes. Over steepened slopes may become gravitationally unstable, leading to a sudden slope failure that result in landslides or debris avalanches. During the eruption of Mt. St. Helens, May 18, 1980, Washington, a debris avalanche was triggered by a magnitude 5.0 earthquake. The avalanche removed the upper 500 m of the mountain, and flowed into the Spirit Lake, raising its level about 40 m. It then moved to the west filling the upper reaches of the North Fork of the Toutle River valley. Debris avalanches, landslides, and debris flows do not necessarily occur accompanied by a volcanic eruption but there are documented cases of such occurrences where no new magma has been erupted.

• **Flooding** - Drainage systems can become blocked by deposition of pyroclastic flows and lava flows. Such blockage can create a temporary dam that could eventually get filled with water and fail resulting in floods downstream from the natural dam. Volcanoes in cold climates can melt snow and glacial ice, rapidly releasing water into the drainage system and possibly causing floods.

• **Tsunami** - Tsunamis occur when eruptions displace ocean water. Debris avalanche events, landslides, caldera collapse events, and pyroclastic flows entering a body of water may generate tsunami.

In 1883 during the eruption of Krakatau volcano, in the straits of Sunda, between Java and Sumatra, several tsunamis were generated by pyroclastic flows entering the sea and by collapse accompanying caldera formation. The tsunami killed about 36,400 people, some even as far away from the volcano as 200 km.

- **Volcanic Earthquakes and Tremors**- Earthquakes usually precede and accompany volcanic eruptions, as magma intrudes and moves within the volcano. Although most volcanic earthquakes are small, some are large enough to cause damage in the area immediately surrounding the volcano, and some others are large enough to trigger landslides and debris avalanches, like in the case of Mount St. Helens. Volcanic Tremor (also called harmonic tremor) can also occur, which is a type of continuous rhythmic shaking of the ground that is generated by magma moving underground.

- **Atmospheric Effects** – Short-term effects on climate are caused when huge quantities of tephra and volcanic gases are injected into the atmosphere. Volcanic ash can cause reflection of solar radiation thereby causing the temperatures to be cooler for several years after a large eruption. The eruption of Tambora volcano in Indonesia in 1813 was the largest in recorded history and the year following the Tambora eruption was known as the "year without summer". Volcanic gases like SO_2 also reflect solar radiation. Also the eruptions in 1981 at El Chichón Volcano, Mexico, and 1991 at Pinatubo, Philippines, ejected large quantities of SO_2 into the atmosphere. A strong El Niño masked the effects of the El Chichón eruption in the year following the eruption, but Pinatubo caused a lowering of average temperatures by about 1°C for two years following the eruption. Volcanic gases like CO_2 are greenhouse gases, which help keep heat in the atmosphere. During the mid-Cretaceous the CO_2 content of the atmosphere was about 15 times higher than present. This is thought to have been caused by voluminous eruptions of basaltic magma on the sea floor. Average temperatures were likewise about 10 to 12°C warmer than present.

- **Famine and Disease** – Wide spread crop damage and death of livestock can be caused by tephra falls leading to famine.

3.8 Predictions and Mitigation of Volcanic Eruption

Volcanic prediction is difficult, but on a comparative scale it is more viable than for earthquakes. The major challenge is that every volcano has unique behaviour, which must be characterized on a case-by-case basis. This is challenging because of the long period of repose between explosions.

Most volcanic predictions are based on various phenomena:

1. Behaviour of the volcano
2. Earthquake activity, tracking the ascent of magma
3. Deformation of the ground surface
4. Changes in the gas chemistry and temperature.

For some volcanoes, the statistical behaviour can be characterized if there is a history of 10-20 eruptive sequences. There is no simple physical theory for the eruptive cycle and this is an empirical approach, Statistical methods give gross probabilities, but not short-time prediction. Individual volcanoes differ in the reliability of earthquake precursors, and again each volcano should be characterized. Inflation of the magma chamber below the volcano causes tilting and uplift of the surface, which can be measured. This is the direct result of ascent of magma and build-up of gas pressure. There are many instances of successful prediction of major eruptions.

1. Long - Term Forecasting

Understanding the geologic history of a volcano is generally necessary to make an assessment of the types of hazards posed by the volcano and the frequency at which these types of hazards have occurred in the past. Once this information is made available, volcanologists can then make forecasts concerning what areas surrounding a volcano would be subject to the various kinds of activity should they occur in a future eruption, and also make forecasts about the long-term likelihood or probability of a volcanic eruption in the area. During such studies, geologists examine sequences of layered deposits and lava flows. With this knowledge about the characteristics of deposits left by various types of eruptions, the past behaviour of a volcano can be determined. Combining this with the radiometric age dating of the deposits the past frequency of events can be determined. This information obtained along with knowledge about the present surface aspects of the volcano are used to make volcanic hazards maps which can aid other scientists, public officials, and the public at large to plan for evacuations, rescue and recovery operations in the event that short-term prediction suggests another eruption. Such hazards maps delineate zones of danger expected from the hazards discussed above: lava flows, pyroclastic flows, tephra falls, mudflows, and floods.

2. Short - Term Prediction

It involves monitoring the volcano to determine when the magma is approaching the surface and monitoring for precursor events that often signal a forthcoming eruption.

• **Monitoring seismic waves** - Since both earthquakes and explosions generate seismic waves, and since S-waves cannot pass through liquids, arrays of seismographs can be placed around a volcano and small explosions can be set off to generate seismic waves. If a magma body exists beneath the volcano, then there will be zone where no S-waves arrive (an S-wave shadow zone) that can be detected. Monitoring the movement of the S-wave shadow zone can delineate the position and movement of the magma body. As magma moves and deforms rocks it may be responsible for the generation of earthquakes. Thus, there is usually an increase in seismic activity prior to a volcanic eruption. Focal depths of these precursor earthquakes may change with time, and if so, the movement of magma can sometimes be tracked. In addition, volcanic tremor is also an indication that magma is moving below the surface.

• **Changes in geophysical signatures** - Rocks contain minerals such as magnetite that are magnetic and these magnetic minerals generate a magnetic field. However, above a temperature called the Curie temperature, these magnetic minerals show no magnetism. So, if a magma body enters a volcano, the body itself will show no magnetism, and if it heats the surrounding rocks to temperatures greater than the Curie temperature (about 500°C for magnetite) the magnetic field over the volcano will be reduced. Thus, by measuring changes in the magnetic field, the movement of magma can sometimes be tracked. Rocks have resistance to the flow of electrical current which is highly dependent on temperature and water content. As magma moves into a volcano the electrical resistivity will decrease. Meâsurements of the electrical resistivity by placing electrodes into the ground, can allow tracking of the movement of magma. As magma approaches the surface or as the temperature of groundwater increases, the amount of surface heat flow will increase. Although these changes may be small they are measured using infrared remote sensing.

- **Changes in ground surface** - As magma moves into a volcano, the structure may inflate causing deformation of the ground surface, which can be monitored. Instruments, like tilt meters measure changes in the angle of the Earth's surface, which are measured in micro-radians. Other instruments are available which track changes in distance between several points on the ground to monitor deformation.

- **Changes in Groundwater System** - As magma enters a volcano it may cause changes in the groundwater system, causing the water table to rise or fall and causing the temperature of the water to increase. By monitoring the depth to the water table in wells and the temperature of well water, spring water, or fumaroles, changes can be detected that may indicate a change in the behaviour of the volcanic system.

- **Changes in chemistry of gases** - The composition of gases emitted from volcanic vents and fumaroles generally changes just prior to an eruption. In general, increases in the proportions of hydrogen chloride (HCl) and sulphur dioxide (SO_2) are seen to increase relative to the proportion of water vapour.

In general, no single event can be used to predict a volcanic eruption, and thus many events are usually monitored and examined in totality, so an eruption can often be predicted. Still, each volcanic eruption is different and until specific patterns are recognized for an individual volcano, predictions vary in their reliability. Also, sometimes a volcano can erupt with no precursor events at all.

Some Case Studies of Volcanic Eruptions

The Volcanic eruption of Mount St. Helens, Montana, USA 1980-resurgence after 123 years

Mount St. Helens had been dormant for 123 years when it suddenly erupted on 18th May, 1980, causing damage exceeding $800 million. Ash-filled steam and gas blasted out horizontally from the mountain at a speed of about 670 miles per hour, destroying about six million trees and scattering them over a 130,000-acre area. Muted by the ash, dust, and fir needles in the air, the sound waves only carried thirty feet. The explosion of the volcano was as large as 500 small atomic bombs, but there were 34 deaths, with 27 others missing. 10,000 animals are estimated to have been killed, along with 15,000 acres of destroyed forestland.

The Volcanic eruption of Mt Pinatubo, Philipines, 1991- alive again after six centuries impacting global warming

On 9th July 1991, the 1,463 metres, dormant volcano near Subic Bay, Mt Pinatubo, Philippine, became active after six centuries with a series of eruptions, which lasted for months. Mt Pinatubo's massive eruption was the largest on record in the Philippines, and in the world for a century since mighty Krakatoa erupted in Indonesia in 1883. By mid-July massive eruptions began and the eruption spewed billions of cubic metres of magma, gases and ash from a three kilometre-long crater near the mountain's summit. The explosive force of the main eruption ejected enormous clouds of ash and gas vertically to an altitude of about 40 km and ash settled deep on the ground over huge areas, up to hundreds of kilometres away. By mid-afternoon 17th July, the sky was as black as night as far south as Manila (85 km away). A continuous 'rain' of pumice pebbles and ash poured down, while thunder and lightning from a tropical storm alternated with brilliant orange flashes from the volcano. There were numerous earthquakes recorded resulting from Pinatubo's continual violent eruptions. As the bulk of its eruptive energy was directed vertically upwards, it did not produce large pyroclastic and molten lava flows that could have devastated towns on the mountain's flanks. The secondary effects, which caused loss of life and property, was due to heavy rains a week later from Typhoon Brenden which sent thousands of tonnes of ash, silt and volcanic debris surging down the mountain. Enormous mud flows and slides wiped many foothill villages, killed many people and forced thousands to flee from their homes. Over the period of eruptions, about 700 died, one million others were forced from their homes (42,000 were destroyed) and 40,000 ha of cropland were buried under ash. Scientists estimated that Pinatubo's eruption added more aerosols than all human-caused 'greenhouse gases' since the industrial revolution. NASA satellites recorded a reduction of up to 1°C in the Earth's average temperature within a year of the main eruption and this cooling effect persisted for about two years, temporarily more than offsetting any global warming effect.

Natural Service Functions of Volcanoes:

Volcanism throughout the entire history of the earth is responsible for outgasing of the Earth to help produce both the atmosphere and hydrosphere. Volcanism renews the soil, and soils around active volcanoes are very fertile. Hydrothermal processes associated with volcanism produce rich ore deposits and the heat rising around magma bodies can sometimes be utilized to produce geothermal energy. The volcanic rocks also provide an abundant local source of materials for landscaping, construction activities and road building. Some volcanoes also provide us natural laboratories for observation of some of the natural processes occurring below the surface of the earth.

When Volcano Erupts

- ⇛Watch out for radio, television and Internet news for warnings.
- ⇛If indoors, close all windows, doors, fire place; switch off all fans, heating and air conditioning systems.

⇛If outdoors, seek shelter indoors.

⇛If caught in a rock fall, roll into a ball to protect your head.

⇛If near a stream or river, be aware of rising water and possible mudflows in low-lying areas. Move up-slope as quickly as possible.

⇛Seek care for burns right away. Immediate care can be life saving.

⇛If your eyes, nose, and throat become irritated from volcanic gases and fumes, move away from the area immediately.

⇛During ash fall, stay inside home, wear long-sleeved shirts/long pants and protect eyes using goggles.

Questions

1. Why do volcanic eruptions occur?

2. Describe the major types of volcanoes, telling which erupt gently and which erupt explosively.

3. Describe the factors controlling the type of volcano.

4. Explain volcanic hazards with suitable examples.

5. How can we predict volcanic eruptions and mitigate volcanic disasters?

6. Write short notes on (a) Factors affecting the formation of volcanoes (b) Beneficial aspects of volcanism.

Some interesting facts

- The steam given off by a volcano is a potential energy source.
- Geothermal energy has provided heating and electricity for more than 90 years in Iceland, New Zealand, and Italy.
- Kilauea, Hawaii, is the world's most active volcano, and it has been erupting continuously since January 3, 1983, with lobes of lava threatening housing subdivisions, and entering the sea through lava tubes. Kilauea rarely erupts from its summit. Instead it erupts from vents on its flanks, particularly along its east and southwest rift zones. The summit of Kilauea is about 4000 feet above sea level. Between 100 and 2000 metric tons of sulphur dioxide (SO_2) are released per day from Kilauea. The rain is so acidic that a desert has formed downwind from the summit of the volcano.
- Mauna Loa Volcano, Hawaii, on the Big Island of Hawaii, is the largest active volcano in the world. It last erupted in 1984. Mauna Loa erupted 14 times in the 20th Century, and 37 times since 1832.
- The name "volcano" is derived from a god of fire in Roman mythology-Vulcan.
- About 1,900 volcanoes are active today or known to have been active in historical times.
- Almost 90 percent of volcanoes are located in the Ring of Fire, a band of volcanoes circling the edges of the Pacific Ocean.
- Volcanoes can rise in subduction zones, areas where plates meet and one is pushed beneath another. Molten rock rises to the surface and forms a volcano.
- Volcanoes can also arise in spreading centres, or rifts, where plates move away from each other, spreading or splitting the Earth's crust.

• Intraplate volcanoes are caused by hot spots deep within the Earth. Magma rises and erupts as lava through cracks in the Earth's surface, forming volcanoes.

• Volcanoes provide valuable mineral deposits and add to fertility of soils.

• The largest volcano in our Solar System is Olympus Mons on Mars. It is about 17 miles (27 km) tall. Mount Everest is about 6 miles (10 km) tall.

• The highest volcano is Ojos Del Salado in Chile. It is 22,589 feet (6,887 m) tall. From base to summit, the tallest would be Mauna Kea, which, when measured from its base on the ocean floor, is more than 30,000 feet high.

• The three countries that have the greatest number of historically active volcanoes are Indonesia, Japan, and the United States in descending order of activity.

• As of the year 2000, USGS scientists estimated that volcanoes posed a tangible risk to at least 500 million people. This is comparable to the entire population of the world at the beginning of the seventeenth century.

• During the 9-hour period of most vigorous activity on May 18, 1980, Mount St. Helens dumped more than 540 million tons of ash over an area of more than 22,000 square miles (56,980 square kilometres). It was the most destructive volcanic eruption known to occur in the United States. Fifty-seven people were killed by the eruption including USGS scientist Dr. David Johnston, who was at a monitoring site 5 miles (8 kilometres) from the volcano. Estimated $1 billion damage was caused by the eruption, through mudflows and landslides as well as what fell from the sky.

Unit 4

WEATHER RELATED HAZARDS

"Humans remain entirely atmosphere dependent, so there is no choice but to respond to extreme climatic behaviour and its many effects"

Peter Garrett

In general, any atmospheric phenomenon that might represent a threat for people, property or environment should be considered as an atmospheric hazard as humans are atmosphere dependent. Any atmospheric changes will affect different parts of the earth to varying degrees. Coastal areas in particular may bear the severe brunt of the extreme weather related hazards like cyclones, tornadoes, hurricanes, storm surges, and droughts. The current population growth trends suggest that by the year 2025 there will be about 8 billion people on the Earth and approximately 66% of them will be living in cities. About 40% of them lie on the coast and therefore are most vulnerable to damages due to extreme weather conditions. With severe weather conditions becoming common globally, research is being done to find ways to reduce the effects of hazardous natural events due to extreme weather conditions on the human population. We cannot stop the geologic process from occurring or suddenly stop the population from growing, but we can only try to predict and attempt to reduce the weather related hazards to life and property. To combat the increasing risk, we need more rigorous scientific research to attempt to understand and help forecast future events. We need to be able to monitor the hazardous events (e.g. meteorological/weather monitoring) and to be able to quickly communicate the information without any scientific jargon from the scientists to the general population.

4.1 Cyclones

Tropical cyclones (known as hurricanes in North America or typhoons in Asia) are giant whirlwinds of air and dense clouds spiralling at approximately 120 km/h around a central 'eye' of extreme low pressure. The average tropical cyclone can last up to a week but it may extend to over three weeks. They develop in the atmosphere over warm ocean areas with at least 26°C water temperature (mainly in latitudes 5° to 20° north or south) although their exact trigger-mechanism is not clear. There are different categories of cyclones depending on the wind gusts.

Categories	Km\hr
I	Strongest wind gusts less than 125 km/h
II	125-169 km/h
III	170-224 km/h
IV	225-279 km/h
V	Wind gusts more than 280 km/h

4.2 Effects of Cyclones

As cyclones approach from the sea they are accompanied with torrential rains, extreme winds and storm surges. The damages caused by each cyclone are determined by its path and can vary greatly. It can damage buildings, crops and boats. Most deaths from cyclones occur as a result of drowning, collapsed buildings, or debris, which become lethal projectiles carried along by the extreme winds.

4.3 Genesis of a Cyclone

The origin of a cyclone is promoted by the following conditions:

- Sea-surface temperatures warmer than 26°C
- Strong low-level cyclonic relative vortices and deep convection over a large area of ocean
- A reasonably large coriolis force to allow an organized circulation to develop

- High relative humidity from the surface upward to above six kilometres
- Spiralling winds at low levels and divergent winds aloft, occurring simultaneously

Cyclone varies greatly in their characteristics but have a common feature that is, a calm centre with a clear sky. This centre, or 'eye' is generally about 16 - 30 km across, but this can also range from 10 - 100 km. Around this eye are bands of heavy clouds, associated with moist air, which spiral in towards the centre of the cyclone. These clouds, known as the 'eye wall', may be 15 km high and mark the ring of strongest winds and heaviest rainfall.

4.4 Behaviour of Cyclones and Their Forecast

Cyclones may last for a few days, to over three weeks and can be predicted, but the path of the cyclone is often uncertain. They need to be tracked continuosly and carefully by meteorologists as they may move forward, backward, stay motionless for periods, or move in circles. When they reach land, the friction of the earth and the loss of sustaining heat energy from the ocean, cause cyclones to 'fill' and drop most of their rain. As cyclones move forward only at 15 – 25 km/ h there is sufficient warning time for people to prepare for the hazard, Every cyclone is dangerous and tropical cyclones are the greatest storms on earth. People in cyclone prone areas need to be aware that if the 'eye' of the cyclone passes over them, there will be a sudden lull in wind and clearing of skies, which may last from a few minutes up to an hour or two. Then the other side of the cyclone will strike and the winds will resume with equal strength, but blowing from the opposite direction. Therefore it is very important that people should remain in shelter during and after the passing of the cyclone 'eye'.

4.5 Factors Affecting Cyclone Hazards

There are numerous factors that can affect the hazards due to cyclones and some of them are mentioned below:

1. Rapid coastal development has led to the destruction of coastal forests during recent years, which has removed a barrier, which

formerly mitigated, to a certain extent the effects of waves and winds from cyclonic storms.

2. Poverty compels people to have protection standards such as housing and infrastructure in an inadequate way for a region subject to frequent intense cyclones.

3. Lack of preparedness and absence of evacuation plans by the local authorities in the cyclone prone regions is a major factor.

4. Anthropogenic effects on the climate also contribute to factors leading to cyclones.

4.6 Structure of a Tropical Cyclone

Converging winds spiral inward towards the central low pressure area, the winds rotate in a counter-clockwise direction around the central low in the northern hemisphere (clockwise in the southern hemisphere). When these winds spiral inward they draw in the thunderclouds around the storm, creating the spiral rain bands that are clearly recorded on the satellite images. As the winds converge toward the central core, they spiral upwards, sending warm moist air upwards. When this air rises, it cools and releases its latent heat into the atmosphere to add further energy to the storm. The winds spiralling around this central core create the eye of the tropical cyclone and eventually spread out at high altitudes. Then, cool air above the eye begins to sink into the central core. This dry descending air within the eye gives the core a clear, cloud free sky, with little to no wind. The main source of energy for the storm is the heat contained in the warm tropical and subtropical oceans, so when the storm moves over the land, it is cut off from its source of heat and will rapidly dissipate.

Winds spiralling counter-clockwise (in the northern hemisphere) into the eye of the hurricane achieve high velocities as they approach the low pressure of the eye. The velocity of these winds is called the hurricane-wind velocity. The central low-pressure centre of the eye also moves across the surface of the Earth as it is pushed by regional winds. The velocity at which the eye moves across the surface is called the storm centre velocity. Hence, for considering the velocity of winds around the hurricane, the wind velocity and the storm centre velocity should be taken into account. These velocities can either add up or subtract depending on the side of the hurricane. Winds are always stronger on the right side of a moving hurricane in the northern hemisphere and in the southern hemisphere, since the winds circulate in a clockwise direction; the winds are stronger on the left-hand side of the storm.

4.7 Size of Tropical Cyclones

Because the winds spiral inward towards the central low-pressure area in the eye of a hurricane, the hurricane-wind velocity increases towards the eye. The distance outward from the eye to which hurricane strength winds occur determines the size of the hurricane. Winds in the eye wall itself have the highest velocity and this zone can extend outward from the centre to distances of 16 to 40 km. Hurricane force winds (winds with velocities greater than 119 km/hr) can extend out to 120 km from the centre of the storm. Some examples of tropical cyclones of different sizes are:

1. The largest tropical cyclone recorded, Typhoon Tip, had gale force winds (54 km/hr), which extended out for 1100 km in radius in the Northwest Pacific in 1979.

2. Hurricane Katrina, in 2005, was a large hurricane with tropical storm force winds extending outward from the eye about 320 km.

3. The smallest, Cyclone Tracy, had gale force winds that only extended 50 km in radius when it struck Darwin, Australia, in 1974.

4.8 Cyclone Risk and Mitigation Strategies

1. Early warning systems are to be installed to give people sufficient time to evacuate them to different places. This could be in the form of alarms or sirens sounded throughout a town, notification by radio, television, Internet and local law enforcement agencies like the police, fire brigade.

2. Meteorological stations around the globe can co-ordinate and track the path of a cyclone and predict when and where the storm will strike. In cyclone-prone regions, infrastructure can be provided to decrease

the damage caused by the cyclones. For example, "cyclone walls" have been built along coastal areas to decrease or stop the impact of a storm surge. These could also be used as roads along which residents can evacuate.

3. Community storm shelters can be built in low-lying coastal areas which can act as evacuation points for people living in the surrounding areas.

4. For successful enforcement of these measures, the population needs to be made aware about the threat of the storms and action plan in case of an emergency.

Case Study of Cyclones

New buildings in Darwin cyclone resistant after Christmas Cyclone Tracy, Australia, 1974

The Cyclone Tracy struck Darwin, Australia early on Christmas morning in the year 1974 causing huge devastations and destroying nearby suburbs. More than sixty-five people were dead or missing at sea. During the storm, most people sheltered deep within their homes and were pierced, crushed or suffocated by their own homes collapsing down, which were poorly designed to withstand a cyclone. Some died outside their homes, deceived by the calm when the eye of the storm passed overhead. These people left their shelters during the brief lull, only to be trapped in the furious winds when the remainder of the cyclone struck. Large offices, flats and schools were the buildings that withstood Cyclone Tracy, which were used to house more than twenty thousand homeless people after the storm had passed. The majority of these people had to be temporarily evacuated from Darwin. When the city was finally planned after the disaster and reconstructed, new buildings were designed to be more cyclone resistant.

4.9 Storm Surge

Cyclone can generate a storm surge or tide, which can be caused by cyclonic winds blowing across the water with a fall in atmospheric pressure. The lower pressure at the eye of the cyclone actually allows a rise in sea level, and close to, the centre. This raised dome of water is usually 60-80 km across and 2 to 5 meters higher than normal sea level. As a cyclone approaches the coast, low-lying areas may experience flooding because strong on-shore winds have displaced the storm surge ahead of the cyclone's centre. The amount of flooding that occurs depends on the height of the tide when the cyclone crosses the coast. If the tide is fairly low, flooding may not occur. The people living in low-lying coastal areas are potentially more at risk from a storm surge than from cyclonic winds. If a storm surge coincides with a high tide, massive flooding and additional destruction is likely to occur. The greatest storm-surge damages lie to the right of a hurricane's eye in the Northern Hemisphere. It occurs to the right of the eye because winds, ocean waves, and sea level rise are all moving in an onshore direction. In contrast, to the left of the eye, ocean waves and sea level rise are moving in an onshore direction, but the winds are blowing in an offshore direction. The offshore direction of the winds moderates the effect of the storm surge.

4.10 Hurricane

Massive tropical cyclonic storms with winds exceeding 119 km/hr are called hurricanes. It forms and intensifies over tropical oceanic regions. In the Atlantic Ocean and eastern Pacific Ocean they are called hurricanes, typhoons in western Pacific, cyclones in the southern hemisphere and all these represent the same process, no matter where they occur. Although death due to hurricanes has decreased in recent years due to better methods of forecasting and establishment of early warning systems, the economic damages from hurricanes have increased as more and more development has taken place along coastal areas. Hurricanes are generally smaller than storms in mid-latitudes, typically about 500 km in diameter.

Case Studies of Hurricanes

Hurricane Elena Cuba, 1985, costs 2.6 billion US dollars

The Hurricane Elena became a hurricane over the southeastern tip of Cuba in 1985. It took a north westward track seeming it would head to New Orleans, but on entering the northern Gulf of Mexico, it turned abruptly towards the east, taking aim on the west coast of Florida. It stalled for about 2 days just south of Pensacola, Florida, and then turned towards the northwest, hitting the coast as a category 3 storm at Biloxi, Mississippi, where it caused damages amounting to approximately $2.6 billion dollars.

Hurricane Andrew, 1992, costs 30 billion US dollars

The Hurricane Andrew in 1992 moved west across southern Florida causing damages worth $30 billion dollars. It weakened a little as it crossed Florida, but on entering the Gulf of Mexico it became stronger, crossed the Gulf and ploughed into south western Louisiana causing an additional $16 billion damages, and killing 26 people along its path.

Deadliest and Costliest Hurricane Katrina, 2005

Hurricane Katrina was one of the costliest and deadliest hurricanes in the history of the United States of America. Katrina originated on 23rd August 2005 causing devastation along much of the north-central Gulf Coast. The most severe loss of life and property damage occurred in New Orleans, Louisiana, which flooded as the levee system miserably failed, hours after the storm had moved inland. Nearly every levee in New Orleans failed as Hurricane Katrina passed east of the city, subsequently flooding 80% of the city and many areas of neighbouring areas for weeks. The hurricane caused severe destruction across the entire Mississippi coast and into Alabama, as far as 160 km from the storm's centre. The storm surge caused severe damage along the Gulf Coast, devastating the Mississippi cities of Waveland, Bay St. Louis, Pass Christian, Long Beach, Gulfport, Biloxi, D'Iberville, Ocean Springs, Gautier, Moss Point, and Pascagoula. About 1,836 people lost their lives in the hurricane and in the subsequent floods, making it the deadliest U.S. hurricane since the 1928 Okeechobee Hurricane. The storm is estimated to have been responsible for $81.2 billion in damage, making it the costliest natural disaster in U.S. history. The hurricane also had a profound impact on the environment. The storm surge caused substantial beach erosion, in some areas completely devastating coastal areas. In Dauphin Island, approximately 15 km to the east of the point where the hurricane made landfall, the sand that comprised the barrier island was transported across the island into the Mississippi Sound, pushing the island towards land. Much of the lands were also which were used as breeding grounds for marine mammals, brown pelicans, turtles, and fish, as well as migratory species such as redhead ducks. Overall, about 20% of the local marshes were permanently overrun by water as a result of the storm. The hurricane also forced the closure of 16 National Wildlife Refuges, of which Breton National Wildlife Refuge received the worst damage, as half of its area was swept off. Finally, as part of the cleanup effort, the flood waters that covered New Orleans were pumped into Lake Pontchartrain, which took approximately 43 days. These residual waters contained a mix of raw sewage, bacteria, heavy metals, pesticides, toxic chemicals, and about 24.6 million litres of oil, which sparked fears in the scientific community of massive numbers of fish deaths.

4.11 Tornadoes

Funnel shaped clouds that are associated with thunderstorms are called tornadoes. A tornado develops within a severe thunderstorm when there is an excessive amount of vertical wind shear. Vertical wind shear is when upper level winds blow at a high velocity relative to lower level winds. Before the development of the thunderstorms strong high level winds that blow to the west initiates a spinning flow near the Earth's surface. This spinning flow takes the form of an invisible horizontally oriented cylinder. As the thunderstorm develops, stronger updrafts of warm air lifts this rotating air into a more vertical position within the thundercloud, causing part of the thundercloud to rotate around the a vortex in a counter clockwise direction. Tornadoes form within this rotating air, usually at the rear flank of the thunderstorm, and extend down from the thundercloud occasionally reaching the surface. Tornadoes have wind velocities higher than hurricanes up to 500 km/hr but affect a much smaller area than hurricanes. They travel at velocities between stationary and 110 km/hr, with cyclonic wind speeds up to 500 km/hr as noted above. The diameters of tornadoes range from a few tens of meters up to 1.5 km. They do not often remain in contact with the ground for long periods of time, but can skip across the surface as the thunderstorm moves along.

Between 1916 and 1990 tornadoes have caused approximately 11,900 deaths in the United States and about 70% of the tornadoes that occur on Earth occur in the great plains of the United States. Damage due to tornado is caused by the high wind speed and high difference in atmospheric pressure between the tornado and its surroundings. The rotating winds can knock down weaker structures, and the extremely low pressure inside the tornado generates strong pressure differences between the inside and outside of buildings. This pressure difference causes roofs to be lifted and removed. The high winds pick up smaller objects including small structures, animals, people, cars, and especially mobile homes, and can carry these objects up to several kilometres. The debris picked up by the winds act as lethal projectiles against a human body. A tornado watch is generally issued for all areas that may fall in the path of the thunderstorm, whenever strong thunderstorm activity is detected, as tornadoes cannot be predicted precisely. Doppler radar can detect rotating motion within a thunderstorm and when this is detected, or a tornado is actually observed, a tornado warning is issued. As tornadoes can strike anywhere and anytime the best mitigation is for people to be aware of the conditions, which lead to tornado development, adhere to any tornado watches or warnings that are issued by a responsible agency, and practise the tornado safety tips. The only other mitigation that can reduce the damage produced by tornadoes is building codes that require structures to be constructed with extra reinforcing of wood frames and masonry.

Service Functions of Hurricanes, Cyclones and Tornadoes

Tropical cyclones bring benefits in the form of essential rain for inland parts of the continents. The dependence of agriculture of all types in the inland areas of the continents is affected by the rainfall produced by decaying tropical cyclones.

When hurricanes, tornadoes and cyclones occur

⇛ Have hurricane straps installed to keep the roofs of houses attached to the walls.

⇛ Storm shutters should be used to protect windows and glass for severe weather. These storm shutters protect against flying debris like tree trunks or other things carried by strong winds.

⇛ Listen to radio and watch television for weather updates and meteorological warnings. If a tornado is coming an underground shelter is best, such as a basement or storm shelter. If you do not have a basement, find a hallway or room away from windows.

⇛ If you are outside and cannot get inside, lie flat in a ditch or ravine. Lie face down and cover your head with your hands.

⇛ If you are in a car, take shelter in a nearby building.

⇛ After a tornado, watch for broken glass and power lines that are downed.

4.12 Thunderstorms

Thunderstorms occur everywhere and are associated with lightning. Lightning can strike people and buildings and can be dangerous. As compared to hurricanes and winter storms, thunderstorms affect relatively small areas. A typical thunderstorm is around 15 miles in diameter and lasts for an average of thirty minutes. Heavy rain from thunderstorms can cause flash flooding and strong winds, hail, and tornadoes are also associated with some thunderstorms. As light travels faster than sound, the lightning is seen before the thunder is heard. We can estimate how many miles away a storm is by counting the number of seconds between the flash of lightning and the clap of thunder and divide the number of seconds by five to get the distance in miles.

Formation of thunderstorms requires three conditions:

1. Moisture availability for cloud formation and rain.

2. Unstable air - relatively warm air that can rise rapidly.

3. Lift - fronts, sea breezes and mountains are capable of lifting air to help form thunderstorms.

Thunder and lightning can sometimes even come with snowstorms. Thunderstorms occur anywhere warm moist air has absorbed sufficient heat to make the air less dense than the surrounding air. This commonly occurs along cold fronts, but can occur in other places as well, particularly where daytime heating forms hot air near the Earth's surface. As the warm moist air rises it begins to cool and water begins to condense into tiny droplets that form clouds. Condensation of the water droplets in the clouds releases the latent heat of evaporation, adding heat to the rising air, thus decreasing its density and allowing it to rise to higher levels in the atmosphere. This rising air, called an updraft, starts to build clouds to heights of up to 6 km. Further rising and cooling within the clouds causes more condensation, as well as the formation of ice crystals which release further latent heat and build cloud heights up to 12 km. Eventually the water droplets and ice crystals in the clouds become so large that they can no longer be supported by the uprising air mass, and they begin to fall forming rapid downdrafts on the leading edge of the cloud. In the mature stage of thunderstorm development updrafts and downdrafts operate side by side within the cloud. This is the most dangerous stage of a thunderstorm because of the high winds accompanying the downdrafts, the heavy rain, as well as thunder, lightning, and possible hail and tornado development. Eventually the cloud reaches the dissipating stage as the downdrafts drag in so much cool dry air that it prevents further updrafts of warm moist air. With lack of updrafts of warm moist air, the cloud begins to dissipate and eventually it stops raining Thunderstorms can form as single cells, with only one cloud mass, or as multiple cells, with several clouds moving along a similar path.

4.13 Hail

Hail is a rain of semi-spherical, concentrically layered ice balls that are dropped from some thunderstorms and range from pea-size stones to grapefruit size stones. Hail rarely kills people but causes heavy damage to agriculture, roofs, and automobiles. The conditions to be met for forming hail during a thunderstorm are:

1. Large thunderstorms with high cloud tops formed from hot moist rising air.

2. Upper level cold air with a large temperature contrast between the upper level air and the rising moist air.

3. Strong updrafts within the thunderstorm to keep hailstones suspended in the cloud while layers of ice are added to the stones. When the stones become too large to be suspended by the cloud they fall to the surface as hail.

Although thunderstorms are most common along the Gulf coast, thunderstorms that produce hail are more common in the mid-continent region where temperature contrasts between upper air masses and the rising hot air are greater.

4.14 Lightning

Lightning is the electrical discharge from clouds, which causes thunder and occurs from all thunderstorms. It is one of the major causes of forest fires and results in many deaths. Lightning is caused by an imbalance of electrical charge between and within clouds and the ground. During the formation of a thundercloud, charged particles of water droplets and ice become separated in the clouds. Positively charged particles move to the top of the cloud and negatively charged particles move to the bottom of the cloud. Then the thundercloud begins to interact with the ground. The negatively charged part of the cloud induces a build-up of positive charges on the ground. Similarly, beneath the upper positively charged part of the cloud negative charges are induced in the ground below. The electricity is discharged as a bolt of lightning, when the difference in voltage between the oppositely charged parts of the cloud and the ground become high enough. The discharge of electricity during a bolt of lightning heats up the air surrounding the bolt causing rapid expansion of the air. It is this rapid expansion of the air that causes the sound which we call thunder. Lightning can travel from the clouds to the ground, from the ground to the clouds, and within the clouds themselves. Lightning travels at speeds of about 100,000 miles per hour, and usually includes several strokes that all occur within about half a second.

Service Functions of Thunderstorms and Lightning

Thunderstorms play a role in the complex balances of the atmospheric circulation, including the global electrical circuit. The benefits include rainfall; scouring of stream and channel beds by sudden deluges; fixing of atmospheric nitrogen for use by plants.

The high temperatures and shock wave due to lightning causes the fixation of atmospheric nitrogen to oxygen molecules, usually as NO, which is then converted to nitric acid in rainwater. Lightning is responsible for about 2% of all the fixed nitrogen supplied to the biosphere.

When lightning strikes

⇛When a storm is heading, look for dark skies, flashes of light or increasing wind. Listen for the sound of thunder. If you can hear thunder, you are close enough to the storm to be struck by lightning. Go to safe shelters immediately. Always find shelter in a building or a car. Keep the car windows closed and avoid convertibles.

⇛Telephone lines and metal pipes can conduct electricity. So unplug appliances and avoid using the telephone or any electrical appliances.

⇛Do not take a bath or shower.

⇛Turn off the air conditioners. Power surges from lightning can overload the compressor and damage the air conditioners.

⇛Draw ventilation blinds and shades over windows.

⇛If you are in the woods, take shelter under the shorter trees.

⇛If you are boating or swimming, get to land and find shelter immediately.

⇛If possible, go to a low-lying, open place, away from trees, poles or metal objects.

4.14 Other Severe Weather Phenomenon

1. **Nor'easters** – Nor'easters, like hurricanes, centres of low pressure with winds that circulate in a counter clockwise direction around the low pressure and are extra tropical cyclonic storms as they originate outside of the tropics. Nor'easters originate in various locations. They are called Nor'easters because the cyclonic circulation causes winds to blow out of the northeast as the storms move up coast. When compared with hurricanes, Nor'easters usually have winds less than hurricane strength (<115 km/hr), but they last several days and can create storm surges up to 7 metres high.

2. **Drought and associated Famine** - In contrast to the exceptional weather conditions like cyclones, tornadoes, hurricanes which tend to bring high quantities of rainfall; a drought is a period of abnormal dryness in a region. A drought is an extended period (of months or years) when a region experiences a noticeable deficiency in water supply and this occurs when a region receives consistently below average precipitations. Droughts, as hazards, are unique in the sense that they are slow onset hazards that may lead to secondary effects like famine. Although droughts can persist for several years, even a short, intense drought can cause significant damage to the local economy and has a substantial impact on the ecosystem and agriculture of the affected region.

Factors Leading to Drought

Rainfall is related to the amount of water vapour in the atmosphere, combined with the upward forcing of the air mass containing that water vapour and if either of these is reduced, the result is a drought. These conditions can be triggered by an above average prevalence of high-pressure systems, winds carrying continental, rather than oceanic air masses, and ridges of high-pressure areas form with behaviours, which prevent or restrict the developing of thunderstorm activity or rainfall over one certain region. Oceanic and atmospheric weather cycles such as the El Niño-Southern Oscillation (ENSO) make drought a regular recurring feature of the Americas along the Pacific coast and Australia. Farming, excessive irrigation, deforestation, and erosion adversely impact the ability of the land to capture and hold water. While the above human activities tend to be relatively isolated in their scope, activities resulting in climate change are expected to trigger droughts with a substantial impact on agriculture throughout the world, and especially in developing countries.

Drought Consequences

It can have significant environmental, agricultural, health, socio-economic consequences and the effect varies according to vulnerability. For example, subsistence farmers are more likely to migrate during drought because they do not have alternative food sources. Some areas with populations that depend on subsistence farming as a major food source are more vulnerable to drought-triggered famine. Drought can also reduce water quality, because lower water flows reduce dilution of pollutants and increase contamination of remaining water sources. Some common consequences of drought include:

1. Decreased crop growth or yield productions and decreased carrying capacity for livestock.

2. Dust bowls, themselves a sign of erosion, further erode the landscapes.

3. Dust storms, when drought hits an area suffering from desertification and erosion.

4. Famine due to lack of water for irrigation, malnutrition, dehydration and other famine related diseases.

5. Habitat and ecosystem damage, affecting both terrestrial and aquatic wildlife.

6. Mass migration resulting in internal displacement.

7. Shortage of water for industrial users.

8. Disputes over natural resources, including water and food and social unrest.

9. Wildfires.

Different Stages Of Drought

Droughts undergo three critical stages before their ultimate manifestation.

1. Meteorological drought precedes the other kinds of drought and occurs when there is an extended period with less than average precipitation.

2. Agricultural droughts are droughts that affect crop production of the region. This condition can also arise independently from any change in precipitation levels when soil conditions and erosion triggered by poorly planned agricultural practices cause a shortfall in water available to the crops. However, in a traditional drought, it is caused by an extended period of below average precipitation.

3. Hydrological drought occurs when the water reserves available in sources such as aquifers, lakes and other reservoirs fall below the statistical average.

Impacts of Drought

Direct impacts include reduced cropland and forest productivity; increased fire hazard; reduced water levels; increased livestock and wildlife mortality rates; and damage to wildlife and fish. Drought impacts can be grouped as economic, environmental, and social.

Economic Impacts

1. Farmers could lose money if a drought destroys their crops or stunts the crops growth, causing lower yields and investing in irrigation or finding new water sources, like wells, loses poor crop quality or money.

2. Ranchers could lose livestock, or they might have to spend more money on feed and water for their animals. People may have to pay more for food products.

3. Businesses that manufacture and sell recreational equipment, like boats and fishing equipment, may not be able to sell some of their goods because drought has dried up lakes and other water sources.

Environmental impacts

Drought also causes adverse environmental impacts- air and water quality reduced because of forest fires; soil erosion; damages to plants, animals, and the ecosystem. Sometimes the damage is only temporary, and conditions return to normal when the drought is over. In some cases, the damages become irreversible if, for example, an endangered species was lost because of low stream flows. Common examples of environmental impacts include the following:

1. Destruction and loss of fish and wildlife habitat, Increase in diseases among wild animals, because of reduced food and water supplies, Migration of wild animals, leading to a loss of wildlife in some areas and too many wildlife in the areas not affected by drought, an increased stress on endangered species.

2. Lower water levels in reservoirs, lakes, and ponds, loss of wetlands.

3. Increased forest fires.

4. Wind and water erosion of soils and decreased soil quality.

Social impacts

They include public safety, health conflicts that arise between people when there is not enough water. Many of the impacts that we consider economic and environmental also have social impacts. Examples of social impacts include:

1. Mental and physical stress due to economic losses caused by drought. Fewer recreational activities. Reduced incomes and migration of populations from rural to urban areas for betterment.

2. Health problems related to reduced water supplies, loss of human life due to heat stress, water shortage.

3. Threat to public safety due to an increased number of forest and range fires.

The above points should be taken into account when planning for and responding to drought conditions.

Strategies for Drought Mitigation

The components of a drought preparedness and mitigation plan are the following:

- Prediction
- Monitoring
- Impact assessment
- Response

1. **Prediction** involves the application of scientific knowledge, such as climate studies and coupled ocean/atmosphere models, survey of snow peaks, anomalous circulation patterns in the ocean and atmosphere, soil moisture, assimilation of remotely sensed data into numerical prediction models, and knowledge of stored water available for domestic, stock, and irrigation uses.

2. **Monitoring** involves the use of ground-based information such as rainfall, weather, crop conditions and water availability coupled with satellite observations for the provision of synoptic, wide-area coverage.

3. **Impact assessment** is done and carried out on the basis of land-use type, persistence of stressed conditions, demographics and existing infrastructure, intensity and areal extent, and its effect on agricultural yield, public health, water quantity and quality, and building subsidence.

4. **Response** includes improved drought monitoring, better water and crop management, augmentation of water supplies with groundwater, increased public awareness and education, watershed and local planning, reduction in water demand, and water conservation.

Drought preparedness and mitigation can be carried out using the following: (1) soil and water conservation, and (2) herd management.

Drought mitigation measures include various techniques that induce rainfall, water conservation and better monitoring practices. Some of the strategies include like cloud seeding (an artificial technique to induce rainfall), desalination of sea water for irrigation or consumption, drought monitoring, water restrictions and usage (using sprinklers, hoses or buckets for outdoor plants, the washing of motor vehicles, cleaning up of swimming pools, and also fitting of water conservation devices), in-situ moisture-conservation practices, Farm management and sustainable strategies, Herd management, Soil and Water Conservation.

Some Case Studies: Drought In India

The Indian agriculture is dependent on the climate of India, which is a favourable southwest summer monsoon as this is critical in securing water for irrigating Indian crops. In certain parts of India, the failure of the monsoons result in water shortages, resulting in below average crop yields. This is particularly true for the major drought-prone regions such as southern and eastern Maharashtra, northern Karnataka, Andhra Pradesh, Orissa, Gujarat, and Rajasthan. In the past, droughts have periodically led to major Indian famines, including the Bengal famine of 1770, in which up to one third of the population in affected areas died; the 1876–1877 famine, in which over five million people died; and the 1899 famine, in which over 4.5 million died. Some of the worst historical droughts that have occurred in the world include:

- 1900 India, killing between 250,000 and 3.25 million people
- 1921-22 Soviet Union, in which over 5 million people died from starvation due to drought
- 1928-30, northwest China, resulting in over 3 million deaths due to famine
- 1936 and 1941, Sichuan Province, China, that resulted in 5 million and 2.5 million deaths
- In 2006, Sichuan Province, China, experienced its worst drought in modern times, with nearly 8 million people and around 7 million cattle facing water shortages

Desertification

Desertification is a land degradation process occurring in arid, semiarid and dry sub-humid areas of the world. Desertification is occurring much faster worldwide than that occurred historically and usually arises from the demands of increased populations that settle on the land in order to grow crops and graze animals. These susceptible dry lands cover 40 percent of the earth's surface and put at risk more than 1 billion people who are dependent on these lands for their survival. A major impact of desertification is biodiversity loss, and loss of productive capacity, such as the transition from grassland dominated by perennial grasses to one dominated by perennial shrubs.

Factors Causing Desertification

• Overgrazing - By pounding the soil with their hooves, livestock compact the substrate, increase the proportion of fine material, and reduce the percolation rate of the soil, thus encouraging erosion by wind and water. Grazing and the collection of firewood reduce or eliminate plants that help to bind the soil.

• Increased population and livestock pressure on marginal lands has accelerated desertification.

• Deforestation practices – Loss of vegetation results in surface run off, as there are no plants to bind the soil and resulting in soil erosion and depletion of nutrients.

The Chipko movement: A mass movement against deforestation

Deforestation is a severe problem in northern India and local people have banded together to prevent commercial timber harvesting. These people have adopted a unique strategy in recognizing trees as valuable, living beings. The Chipko Movement, led by Sunderlal Bahuguna, began in 1973 in the village of Mandal in the upper Alakananda valley with the thought of embracing the trees and was called as tree huggers. Women took their children to the forests and formed a circle around the trees to prevent the slaughtering of trees. The peasants of India's hills depend on the forests for fuel, fodder, and agricultural implements, building timber, medicines and in times of dearth, food. The Chipko people believed that the trees were living and breathing carbon dioxide, and the trees should be respected. The extensive forests were central to the successful practice of agriculture and animal husbandry. In addition, medicinal herbs were used for healing powers. The success of Chipko has saved some 100,000 trees from excavation.

Famine

Famine refers to the complete absence of food and is manifested by - malnutrition, starvation, population explosions and natural disasters. Some important causes include:

1) Natural disasters like floods, drought, desertification, volcanic eruptions and earthquakes.

2) Some areas that are densely overpopulated and are unable to feed masses of people due to population explosion.

3) Poor or low quality of health facilities and improper manage of resources by governments.

The world's countries are divided into developed countries, developing and under developed countries. For example, the richer countries (like Great Britain, France, Australia, Japan and the USA) are usually referred to as the first world countries and those that are poorer (such as Ethiopia, Bangladesh, Cambodia and Sudan in Africa) are referred to as third world countries. A lot of the famine and starvation occurs in the third world countries because of over population, desertification, drought – like conditions and insufficient money, resources and health facilities to keep their people well-fed and healthy.

El Nino

El Niño – Southern Oscillation commonly referred to as ENSO is a global coupled ocean-atmosphere phenomenon. The two important temperature fluctuations in surface waters of the tropical Eastern Pacific Ocean are the El Niño and La Niña. El Niño, means "the little boy" in Spanish, and refers to the Christ child, because this phenomenon is usually noticed around Christmas in the Pacific Ocean off the west coast of South America. La Niña means "the little girl" and is just like the El Nino. These effects were first described in the year 1923 by Sir Gilbert Thomas Walker and are an important aspect of the Pacific ENSO phenomenon, is named after him. The atmospheric signature, the Southern Oscillation (SO) reflects the monthly or seasonal fluctuations in the air pressure difference between Tahiti and Darwin, Australia. The most recent occurrence of El Niño was observed in September 2006, which lasted until early 2007. The phenomenon is associated with droughts, floods, and other disturbances in different locations around the world. Predictions of El Ninos are very interesting because of their irregularity and the effects caused. During major warm events, El Niño warming extends over much of the tropical Pacific and becomes clearly linked to the intensity of the Southern Oscillation. Basically the effects are observed between the Pacific and Indian Oceans, but it also causes effects in the Atlantic Ocean lag behind those in the Pacific by 12 to 18 months. The countries mostly affected by El Ninos are the developing countries, largely dependent upon their agricultural lands and fisheries for food supply, employment, and foreign exchange.

The following are the first signs observed when an El Niño occurs:

1. Increase in air pressure above the Indian Ocean, Indonesia, and Australia.

2. Decrease in air pressure above Tahiti and the rest of central and eastern Pacific Ocean.

3. Weakening of trade winds in the south Pacific.

4. Warm air rises near Peru that causes rain in the northern Peruvian deserts.

5. Warm water spreads from the west Pacific and the Indian Ocean into the east Pacific. It takes the rain along with it, causing extensive droughts in the western Pacific and rainfall in the usually dry eastern Pacific.

Effects of El Nino conditions

El Nino can cause increased rainfall across the east-central and eastern Pacific Ocean.

1. They are associated with warm and very wet summers along the coasts of northern Peru and Ecuador causing major floods when the phenomenon is strong.

2. Another direct effect of El Niño is the occurrence of dry conditions in parts of South East Asia, Northern Australia that results in increased occurrence of forest fires decreasing the air quality and causing pollution.

3. Increased sea ice is observed in the west of the Antarctic Peninsula, the Ross, Bellingshausen and Amundsen Sea sectors.

4. El Ninos can cause destruction to the coral reefs that are sensitive ecosystems, which are a home to many plants and fish. The increase in sea temperature caused by El Ninos destroys algae, which protect the coral, which eventually bleaches white and dies. The destruction of coral reefs from the effects of El Nino can be quite extensive. And the recovery of the reefs can take a very long time.

5. The fishing sectors and industries along the whole coastline can be affected thereby affecting the food supplies, employment and economy.

Human Induced Atmospheric Hazards: Climate Change, Acid Rain and Ozone Depletion

Climate Change

Climate change refers to the changes in the long-term climate or changes in the average weather for a particular location and can result from natural processes, such as the change in the sun's strength, or from human activities, through the build-up of greenhouse gases. The most important concern is with the concentrations of the greenhouse gases, which act as a blanket and trap the heat that comes from the earth. The atmospheric concentrations of these gases have increased significantly since pre-industrial times largely because of fossil fuel usage, decrease in forest cover, etc., resulting in climate change. This blanket effect is natural and a very important part of life on earth.

The release of chlorofluorocarbons and other atmospheric pollutants depletes stratospheric ozone, which, in turn, increases human exposure to ultraviolet radiation, causing skin cancer and cataracts. The recognition of direct effects on human health was a major stimulus to the Montreal Protocol (1987), which acts to reduce emissions of pollutants that weaken the ozone layer. Although this international agreement is proving highly effective in reducing risks in the long term, UV radiation remains a health hazard. The World Health Organization and partner organizations - through the Intersun project - have developed and promote the UV Index, a tool to inform and educate the public about sun protection.

Global Warming and Greenhouse Effect

Energy received from the sun warms up the earth's surface. As this energy passes through the atmosphere, a certain percentage (about 30%) gets scattered. Some part of this energy is reflected back into the atmosphere from the land and ocean surface. The rest (70%) remains to heat the earth in order to establish a balance; the earth must radiate some energy back into the atmosphere. As the earth is much cooler than the sun, it does not emit energy as visible light but emits through infrared or thermal radiation. Some of the gases in the atmosphere, which form a sort of blanket around the earth, absorb some of this energy emitted back into the atmosphere. Our earth would be around 30°C colder than it normally is without this blanket effect. Gases like carbon dioxide, methane, and nitrous oxide, along with water vapour, comprise less than one per cent of the atmosphere and are called 'greenhouse gases' as the working principle is same as that which occurs in a greenhouse (Figure 4.1). The greenhouse gas layer functions similar to a green glass house, where the glass allows sunlight to come in but prevent the heat from going out. Glass easily transmits short wave length solar energy into the greenhouse and is almost opaque to the longer wavelengths radiated by the interiors of the greenhouse. This trapping of the radiation is responsible for the increased temperatures inside the greenhouse. This phenomenon is known as the green house effect and this process results in warming the air in the lower layers leading to global warming. This gas blanket has been in place ever since the origin of the earth. After the industrial revolution, human activities have been releasing more of these greenhouse gases into the atmosphere leading to the thicker blanket and upsetting the 'natural greenhouse effect'. The resulting enhanced greenhouse effect is more

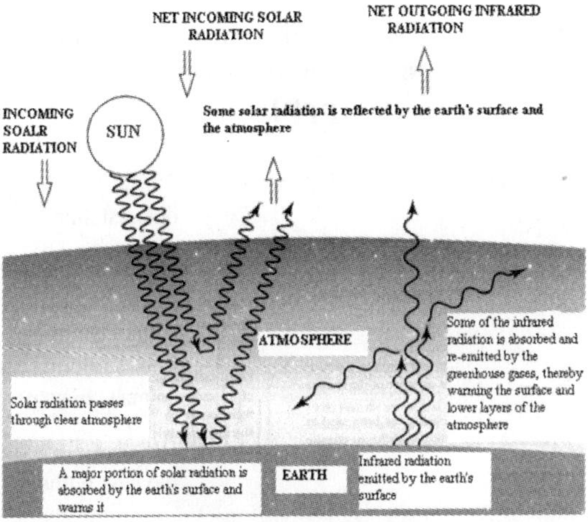

Figure 4.1 Greenhouse effect

commonly referred to as global warming or climate change. The most important green house gases are CO_2, methane, chlorofluorocarbons and nitrous oxide. Scientists predict that temperatures would increase up to 1.5 - 4.5°C by 2100 and may cause glaciers to melt, sea levels rise, and redistribution of dry and wet regions.

During the pre-industrial era, the amount of carbon dioxide remained constant but now it has increased from 250 ppm (1900) to approximately 350 ppm due to industrialization and urbanization. Economic activity, technology and population explosion are driving factors in enhancing global warming. Atmospheric CO_2 levels have been increasing at an alarming rate since 1970. 100 years back the CO_2 level was just 275 ppm, now it is approximately 350-370 ppm and is expected to reach 450 ppm by the year 2040. This will result in an enormous increase in the earth's temperature. The Kyoto Protocol formulated in December,

1997, in Kyoto, Japan, focused on reducing carbon emissions by 50% or to the pre-1990 levels.

Table 4.1 The Major greenhouse gases, their sources and atmospheric concentration

Major Green house Gases	Atmospheric concentration (ppb)	Sources
Carbon dioxide (CO2)	375,000	Fossil fuel combustion, deforestation
Methane (CH_4)	1,850	Swamps, marshes, paddy fields, wetlands, livestock, natural gas leaks, fermentation from enteric processes of animals, biomass burning
Nitrous oxide (N_2O)	316	Fertilizers, fossil fuels, biomass burning
Chlorofluorocarbons and halocarbons	1.2	Aerosols, plastic foams, industrial solvents, air conditioning, refrigeration

Climate scientists predict that the greenhouse gases will increase the global average temperatures by approximately 6 degrees Fahrenheit by the end of this century. Also extreme floods, droughts and heat waves, are likely to occur with increasing frequencies. The University of Wisconsin, Madison and WHO team, predict the following changes according to their model-based forecasts:

• Climate-related disease risks of the various health outcomes are likely to double by 2030.

• Floods as a result of coastal storm surges will affect the lives of approximately 200 million people by the 2080s.

• Heat related deaths in California are likely to more than double by 2100.

• The hazardous ozone pollution in the Eastern U.S. may increase to 60 percent by 2050.

It is predicted that the regions at highest risk of the health effects of climate change include coastlines along the Pacific, Indian oceans and sub-Saharan Africa. Africa has the lowest per-capita emissions of greenhouse gases but is at risk for diseases related to global warming. Some of the many important diseases in poor countries, like malaria, diarrhea and malnutrition, are highly sensitive to climate.

Environmental Impacts of Greenhouse Gases and Global Warming

A rise in temperature would lead to the following consequences:

• Rapid loss of biodiversity and a decline in natural resources.

• Change in the rainfall and monsoon patterns, melting of ice caps and glaciers.

• Increasing temperatures would cause thermal expansion of the oceans and the sea level will rise. This will result in floods in the productive deltaic regions. Sea level rise can result in the disappearance of many islands in the Caribbean, Pacific and the Indian oceans. Climate change can cause disastrous effects on the ecosystems and disruption of marine ecosystems, flooding of the coastal wetlands.

• It could result in frequent storms in many regions where storms were never experienced before and floods can result in the spread of infectious diseases and groundwater can be contaminated.

Acid Rain

Another common human induced atmospheric hazard is acid rain. When rainwater goes below a pH of 5.6, it is called acid rain as normal rainwater has a pH of 5.6 due to the dissolution of CO_2 in rainwater. The phenomenon occurs when sulphur dioxide and nitrogen oxides from the burning of fossil fuels such as, petrol, diesel, and coal combine with water vapour in the atmosphere and fall as acidic rain, snow or fog. These gases can also be emitted from natural sources like volcanoes. Acid rain causes extensive damage to water, forest, soil resources and even human health. They can be wet depositions, where the acidic substances are dissolved in rain, dew, fog, snow and dry depositions, where acidic particulate matter in dry form can be deposited on vegetation, monuments, etc. Acid rain mobilizes heavy metals like cadmium, mercury, calcium, etc., in soils, rocks, sediments that are slowly leached and enter the surface of water bodies. Many lakes and streams have been contaminated and this has led to the disappearance of some species of fish in Europe, USA and Canada as also extensive damage to forests and other forms of life. It can corrode buildings, monuments and be hazardous to human health. Because the contaminants are carried long distances, the sources of acid rain are difficult to pinpoint and hence difficult to control. For example, the acid rain that may have damaged some forest in Canada could have originated in the industrial areas of USA.

The Adirondack Park acid rain: 200 times more acidic than natural rain

The Adirondack Park, which is located in New York, suffered the worst damage from acid rain. About 500 lakes and ponds (out of 2,800) in the Adirondack Park are already too acidic to support the plants and aquatic wildlife that once existed in them. Utility plant pollution from the highly industrial Midwest states of Ohio, Illinois, Indiana and Pennsylvania, is carried Northeast by wind patterns. As the winds rise over the Adirondack Mountains, the moisture which they contain cools and condenses into clouds. The moisture, saturated with heavy amounts of nitric and sulphuric acid, precipitates onto the Adirondack Mountains, damaging the vegetation. Precipitation can be more than 200 times more acidic than natural rain, with a pH of 3.3 or less.

Ozone Layer Depletion

Ozone layer depletion is another important human induced atmospheric hazard. Ozone is a triatomic form of oxygen and is a strong oxidant. It derives its name from the Greek word ozein meaning smell as it has a pungent smell in a concentrated form. About 90 % of the ozone in the atmosphere is present in the stratosphere and this protective ozone is formed as a product of a photochemical equilibrium. Ozone is being continuously formed in the stratosphere by the absorption of short wavelength ultraviolet radiation and is also removed by chemical reactions converting it back to molecular oxygen. Ozone formation in the stratosphere is described by the following reactions:

$$O_2 + h\gamma \rightarrow O + O$$

$$O + O_2 + M \rightarrow O_3 + M$$

Where, M represents a third body (N_2 or O_2) necessary to carry away the energy released in the reaction and hγ is the ultraviolet radiation in this reaction having wavelength less than 242 nm. Opposing the above formation process is ozone removal by photo dissociation:

$$O_3 + h\gamma \rightarrow O_2 + O$$

Wherein ozone absorbs UV-radiation in the 200 - 320 nm wavelength regions. The above combination of reactions form a long chain in which oxygen atoms are constantly being shuttled back and forth between various molecular forms. The net effect of the above reactions is the creation of a layer of ozone in the stratosphere. The balance between creation and removal is affected by increasing stratospheric concentrations of chlorine, nitrogen and bromine, which act as catalysts speeding up the removal process. The most prominent ozone destructive gases are the CFCs that are very stable compounds, relatively unaffected by the usual pollutant removal process in the troposphere. CFC molecules can be broken by ultraviolet radiation freeing the chlorine that is available to destroy ozone. For example, the reaction involving CFC-12 is as follows:

$$CCl_2F_2 + h\gamma \rightarrow Cl + CClF_2$$

Ozone can be removed from the stratosphere by catalytic reactions involving chlorine, nitrogen, hydrogen oxides or bromines. It is the enhancement of these reactions by anthropogenic activities that are of concern. Catalytic destruction of ozone can be explained with the help of the following reactions:

$$X + O_3 \rightarrow XO + O_2$$

$$XO + O \rightarrow X + O_2$$

$$O + O_3 \rightarrow O_2 + O_2$$

Where X may be Cl, Br, OH or NO. The net result of this pair of reactions is the destruction of ozone molecule. Stratospheric ozone depletion refers to the destruction of the earth's ozone layer and thereby reducing its ability to shield ultraviolet (UV) radiation from the Earth's surface.

Ultraviolet radiations are of three kinds UV-A, UV-B and UV-C, among which UV-B is known to be most harmful to biological systems. The ozone layer present in the stratosphere filters out the harmful UV-B radiations from the Sun, thereby protecting life on our earth. This UV-B has disastrous effects on humans, animals, vegetation and the environment by causing DNA damage resulting in humans and animals - mutations, eye cataracts and cancers, Plants – reduction of yield in crops like sorghum, rice, cotton, wheat, soybeans etc, Materials – degradation of paints and plastics.

Pollutants, such as chlorofluorocarbons (CFCs), released from refrigeration, air conditioning systems, solvents, plastic foams, aerosols, propellants destroy this equilibrium and the ozone (O_3) present in the stratosphere. The result is the thinning of the ozone layer, particularly at the poles. In addition to reducing ozone concentrations, CFCs are themselves potent greenhouse gases and trap an enormous amount of heat. In addition, the supersonic aircrafts flying at stratospheric heights can cause major disturbances in the ozone layer. In spite of the slow vertical mixing of pollutants some of the pollutants like CFCs enter the stratosphere and remain there for many years until they are converted to other products. They stay for about 60 -100 years in the stratosphere. This results in depletion of the layer. The Montreal Protocol on Substances that Deplete the Ozone Layer (1987) listed the substances that cause depletion of the ozone and called for about 50% reduction of CFCs by the year 2000.

What can be done by individuals to reduce global warming and the resultant climate change

A major part of our energy requirement is met from fossil fuels (oil, coal and gas) and any actions that reduce energy use will reduce the emissions of carbon dioxide.

• When you buy a car or scooter or any vehicle dependent of fossil fuel, choose one that gets good mileage. Carpool or drive less. Use vehicles that have catalytic converters fitted, which reduce the emission of pollutants.

• Insulate and weatherise your home or apartment during winters to save electricity consumption. Turn off lights and appliances when not needed.

• Replace old, worn-out appliances (e.g., refrigerators, heat pumps) with the most efficient new models.

• Plant trees.

• Reduce, Reuse and Recycle.

• Get interested in the issues involved and help your family and friends to understand the seriousness about climate change. Also, actively support the government policies that support actions reducing climate change effects.

Questions

1. Write short notes on
    - Cyclones
    - Hurricanes
    - Tornadoes
    - Storm surge
    - Thunderstorms
2. Explain how a cyclone is formed.
3. Describe the origin and formation of hurricanes.
4. How can we mitigate cyclone and hurricane disasters?
5. How can we predict a cyclone?
6. Discuss global warming and its effects.
7. Discuss acid rain, its causes and effects.
8. What do you understand by Ozone hole? Explain its effects.

Some Interesting Facts

- Tornadoes have been reported in Great Britain, India, Argentina, and other countries, but most tornadoes occur in the United States.
- Tornadoes form when warm, humid air collides with cold, dry air.
- Once a tornado hits the ground, it may last for as little as a few seconds or as long as three hours.
- Hurricanes can cause floods, flash floods, tornadoes, and landslides.
- Storm surge, an abnormal rise in sea level, is usually the most dangerous part of a hurricane. Surges can cause beach erosion, wash out roads, and decimate homes.
- Lightning often strikes outside of heavy rain and may occur as far as 10 miles away from any rainfall.
- The steel frame of a hard-topped vehicle provides increased protection during lightning if we do not touch the metal. Although you may be injured if lightning strikes your car, you are much safer inside a vehicle than outside.
- Lightning-strike victims carry no electrical charge and should be attended to immediately.

• About 100 lightning strikes occur worldwide every second. During any given minute, there are more than a thousand thunderstorms around the Earth causing some 6,000 flashes of lightning. A lot of it goes from cloud-to-cloud.

• There are worse weathers in other planets on the solar system. Mars can whip up hurricane-like storms four times bigger than Texas. Dust storms on the red planet can obscure the entire globe! Jupiter has a hurricane twice the size of our entire planet, and it has lasted for at least three centuries. Venus is a living hell, and Pluto is routinely more frigid than the coldest place on Earth.

• Mt. Cotopaxi in Ecuador supports the only glacier on the equator.

• At any particular time, there are approximately 1,800 thunderstorms occurring in the Earth's atmosphere.

• Thunderstorms can generate gusts of wind that can develop additional thunderstorms 100 miles away.

• Approximately 1/3 of the Earth's land surface is desert. This is arid land with meagre rainfall that supports only sparse vegetation and a limited population of people and animals. These arid regions are called deserts because they are dry. Some deserts are hot, and some are cold. They may be regions of sand or vast areas of rocks and gravel peppered with occasional plants. But all deserts have very little precipitation.

• Antarctica, the coldest place on earth, is almost entirely covered in ice.

• The largest hailstone ever, was found in Kansas, USA. It was the size of a melon, 19cm wide and weight 758gms.

• The largest desert in the world is the Sahara Desert in Africa, it is almost as large as the United States but the driest desert on Earth is the Atacama Desert in Chile. This desert is virtually rainless with an average rainfall of 1 mm. per year only. It is 50 times more arid than California's Death Valley. The coldest desert during winter is the Gobi Desert in China.

• McMurdo Dry Valleys are the coldest desert system in the world. They represent 2% of the Antarctic continent that is free from ice. High winds can reach -32 F. There can be seasons of complete darkness or light, which makes it a difficult environment for life. When first discovered, the valley was referred to as the Valley of the Dead. Winds can reach an excess of 200 mph, which can evaporate water, ice, and snow.

• Dasht-e Lut in Iran is a large salt desert. It is 300 miles long, and 200 miles wide. It is one of the hottest and driest deserts, with NASA having recorded a satellite surface temperature of 159 F.

• Thar desert is the seventh largest desert in the world. It is very inhospitable. About 4,000 years ago, it contained one of the oldest civilizations, the Mohenjo Daro and Harappa, located in India. Here, the day temperatures can be very high, and drop to below freezing at night. About 10% of the land is comprised of dunes, while the rest is rock, salt-lake bottoms, and interdunal and fixed dune areas.

• Over 90% of Libya is desert.

• Sahara is the world's largest hot desert, running through 11 countries. It covers most of Northern Africa. It is larger than Australia, and nearly as large as the United States. It is nearly 3 million years old. The hottest temperature recorded here was 136 F, yet the temperature can drop below freezing at night.

• The tornado is the most violent of all earth's storms.

• In 1967, Hurricane Beulah unleashed 115 tornadoes over Texas.

• One lightning bolt has enough electricity to service 200 000 homes.

• It is reported that a baseball-sized hail killed 246 people in India in 1888.

• Thunderstorms can generate gusts of wind that can develop additional thunderstorms 100 miles away. Supercells are the most dangerous types of thunderstorms.

• The windiest place in the world is Port Martin, Antarctica, which has an average wind speed over a year of 64 km/h (40 mph). It experiences gale force 8 winds for over a hundred days a year!

• The most violent tornado in recorded history struck on 18 March 1925, killing 689 people, injuring 1980 others, destroying 4 towns, severely damaging 6 others and leaving 11,000 homeless across Missouri, Indiana and Illinois.

• The fastest winds on earth are inside a tornado funnel. Winds here have been recorded at 480 km/h (300 mph).

• The Australian wind record goes to Mardie in Western Australia, when winds gusted to 259 km/h (162 mph) during Cyclone "Trixie" on 19th February 1975.

• The strongest wind gust recorded on the surface of the earth is 371km/h (231 mph) at Mount Washington, New Hampshire (USA) on 12th April 1934.

• Cloud droplets are extremely small. They are about ten thousandth of an inch across, a thousand times smaller than a raindrop.

• The largest piece of ice to fall to earth was an ice block 6 metres (20 ft) across that fell in Scotland on 13th August, 1849.

• The tiny droplets of water that make up fog are so small that it would take seven thousand million of them to make a single tablespoonful of water.

• Waterspouts are simply tornadoes that exist over a body of water. They are often much weaker than land-based twisters due to atmospheric differences. Waterspouts are able to pick up the water and swirl it in its funnel. In some occasions, waterspouts have picked up tadpoles, lizards and fish, which eventually rained down from the sky once the waterspout diminished. These forces of nature often occur in tropical regions where there are oceans and lakes but can also occur in less tropical areas such as the Great Lakes. Ships out on the open seas have reported seeing up to as many as 30 waterspouts in one day!

• One of the most famous droughts occurred during the 1930s and lasted nearly a decade. The Dust Bowl also popularly called the Dirty Thirties was a period of severe dust storms causing great ecological and agricultural damage to American and Canadian prairie lands from 1930 to 1936. It was caused by a combination of drought and poor farming practices. Large areas of land without groundcover allowed winds to blow dust everywhere.

• Between Spring and early Fall 2002, moderate to extreme drought conditions over large portions of 30 states resulted in an estimate of more than $ 10.0 billion in damages and costs.

• In 1980, a combined Drought and Heat Wave between June and September through much of Central and eastern U.S. resulted in an estimated $20.0 billion damage and costs to agriculture and other related industries and an estimated 10,000 deaths including those related to heat.

• Global warming is not only a threat to our future health, it already contributes to more than 150,000 deaths and 5 million illnesses annually, according to a team of health and climate scientists at the World Health Organization and the University of Wisconsin at Madison—and those numbers could double by 2030. Research data published in the journal Nature show that global warming may affect human health in a surprising number of ways: speeding the spread of infectious diseases such as malaria and dengue fever; creating conditions that lead to potentially fatal malnutrition and diarrhea; and increasing the likelihood of heat waves and floods.

• In ancient times, houses in parts of western Rajasthan were built so that each had a rooftop water harvesting system. Rainwater from these rooftops was directed into underground tanks. This system can be seen even today in all the forts, palaces and houses of the region.

• Deserts threaten more than one third of the African continent. The main cause of desertification is not drought but mismanagement of land, overgrazing, felling of trees and for fuel.

• Each year an estimated 5 to 7 million hectares of agricultural land are lost to erosion.

• 84% of agricultural land in eastern Canada is polluted by acid rain. Trees in eastern Canada are dying. The tops of trees like spruce, fir and pine turn yellow, their growth slows down, sometimes the bark splits and finally the tree dies. 80% of Canadians live in areas where acid rain levels are above acceptable levels. Acid rain has also been linked to respiratory diseases in children. Buildings are being affected, especially those made of marble, granite and limestone. Some estimates suggest that buildings in Canada are losing 4% of their weight every year.

Unit 5

FLOODS

"Great floods have flown from simple sources."

William Shakespeare

Water is constantly moving within and above the earth in a cycle called hydrological cycle. Even additional small amounts of precipitation more than the average amounts can cause a stream to run out of its confines and submerge surrounding areas i.e. flooding. Rivers and streams are natural sources of water for consumption, agriculture, and industry. Streams also provide transportation routes, energy, and a means of waste disposal. Stream valleys offer a relatively flat area for constructions. Throughout the history of the growth of civilizations, humans have found it advantageous to construct cities along streams. But, human populations that live along and near the streams also have to face the threat that the flow of water in streams is never constant. High amounts of water flowing in streams can often lead to flooding, and is one of the most common and costly types of natural disasters.

The various reasons for flooding can be that during heavy rainfall the rivers overflow its bank or when ocean waves come onshore or when snow melts rapidly or when dams or levees fail. Flooding can be only a few inches of water or it may cover a house to the rooftop. Floods that happen very quickly are called flash floods. A flood results when a stream runs out of its confines and submerges surrounding areas. Flat or nearly flat land adjacent to a stream or river that experiences occasional or periodic flooding is the flood plain (Figure 5.1, 5.2), which consists of floodway (stream channel and adjacent areas that carry flood flows) and the flood fringe (areas covered by the flood which do not experience a strong current).

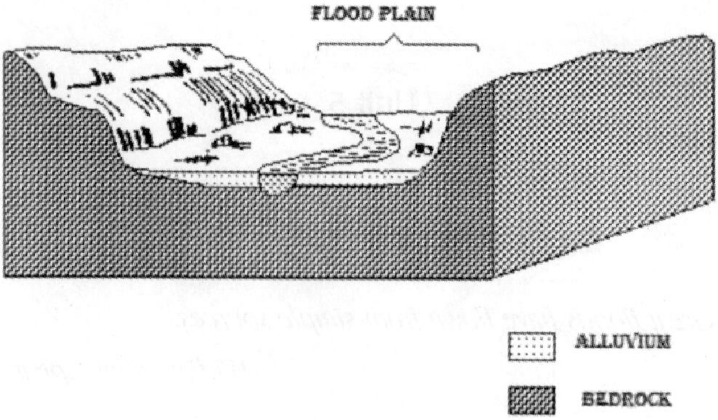

Figure 5.1 Flood plain

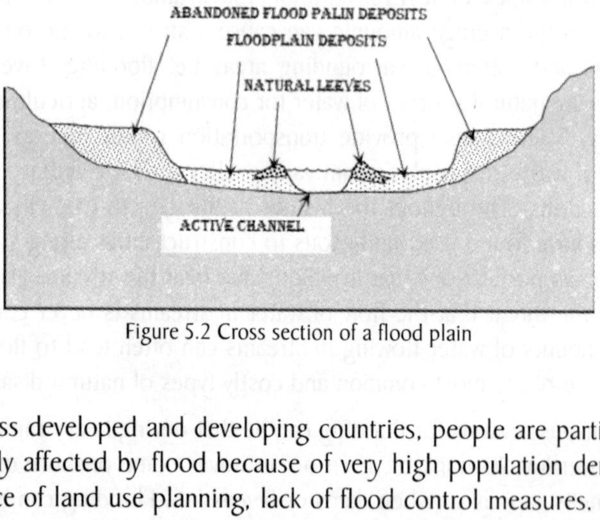

Figure 5.2 Cross section of a flood plain

In less developed and developing countries, people are particularly severely affected by flood because of very high population densities, absence of land use planning, lack of flood control measures, lack of emergency response and training, lack of early warning systems. For example, Bangladesh is one of the most vulnerable countries to flood disasters as about one-half of the land area in Bangladesh is at an elevation of less than 8 metres above sea level. 30% of the country has been covered with floodwaters and in 1991 more than 200,000 deaths resulted from flooding and associated tropical cyclones.

Contrastingly, in the developed countries, the loss of life is usually lower because of proper flood control structures, strict zoning regulations that prevent the habitation of seriously vulnerable lands, and emergency preparedness. Engineering solutions such as levees, bunds, reservoirs, and weirs are used to prevent flooding. Coastal flooding has been addressed by constructing sea walls and artificial beach nourishment in Europe. For example, London is protected from flooding by a huge mechanical barrier, the Thames barrier, across the River Thames, which is raised when the water level reaches a certain point. Venice has a similar arrangement, although it is already unable to cope with very high tides. There are, of course, always reports of property damage and disruption of life. Despite the availability of flood control structures and proper land use planning, floods still do occur and disrupts normal life.

People, who live near rivers and in low-lying coastal areas, live with the greatest threat of floods. Periods of heavy rain, not necessarily in their area, can lead to rises in the water level of streams and rivers to a point where channels can no longer hold the volume of water. Alternatively, for some coastal dwellers, there is the threat from the sea.

5.1 Different Kinds of Floods

Floods can be rapid or slow. It could also be classified as riverine, estuarine, coastal, catastrophic or muddy floods.

Table 5.1 Different kinds of floods

Riverine floods	Heavy rains from monsoons, hurricanes and tropical depressions causes riverine floods, which are slow, but rapid riverine flooding is caused by intense thunderstorm.
Estuarine floods	Storm force winds generate sea tidal surges, which can flood estuarine areas.
Coastal floods	Tsunami, hurricanes and severe sea storms are known to flood coastal areas.
Catastrophic floods	Catastrophic events like earthquakes, volcanic eruptions and dam failure cause these types of floods.
Muddy floods	Runoffs on croplands can result in muddy floods.

5.2 Factors Leading to Floods

Floods have been occurring throughout history of the earth and can be expected as long as the hydrological cycle operates. Streams receive most of their water input from precipitation, and the amount of precipitation falling in any given drainage basin varies on a daily, yearly and centennial basis. Thus, from a geological point of view, floods are a natural consequence of stream flow in a continually changing environment.

1. Precipitation

Weather patterns determine and control the amount and location of rain and snowfall. The amount and time over which precipitation occurs is variable for any given area. Overall, the water cycle is a balanced system. Though water flowing into one part of the cycle is balanced by water flowing back to the ocean, sometimes the amount flowing in to one area is greater than the capacity of the system to hold it within natural confines, which results in a flood. Combinations of various factors along with exceptional precipitation can also lead to flooding. For example, heavy snow melts, water saturated ground, unusually high tides, and drainage modifications when combined with heavy rain can result in flooding.

2. Coastal Flooding

Areas along coastlines get subjected to flooding as a direct result of tsunamis, hurricanes and unusually high tides. In addition, long-term processes like subsidence and rising sea level as a result of global warming can lead to the encroachment of the sea on to the land.

3. Dam and Levee Failures

Dams can be either natural or human constructed features. Natural dams are created by natural processes like volcanic events (lava flows and pyroclastic flows), landslides, or blockage by ice. Human constructed dams are built with a single purpose or with multiple purposes like water storage, generation of electrical power and flood control. All types of dams may fail with the sudden release of water into the downstream drainage. Spectacular and devastating examples of dam and levee failures that results in flooding downstream include:

• The St. Francis Dam near Saugus, California, failed in 1929, killing 450 people.

• The Johnstown, Pennsylvania dam, built of earthen material (soil and rock) collapsed after a period of heavy rainfall in 1889. The flood killed 2,200 people.

• The Vaiont Dam in Italy did not fail in 1963, but the landslides that moved into the reservoir behind the dam caused water to overtop the dam killing over 3,000 people.

• During the Hurricane Katrina in New Orleans (August 2005), levee systems designed to prevent flooding failed and lead to catastrophic flooding and loss of life.

5.3 Factors Affecting Flooding

The main factors that cause flooding are heavy rainfall, sudden or heavy snowmelt, and dam failure. All of these factors can suddenly increase discharge of water into streams, within streams, and out of streams. Furthermore, when the discharge causes the river to rise above flood stage water runs onto the floodplain. The main cause of flooding is heavy rainfall over a short period of time.

When rain falls on the surface of the Earth, some part of the water is evaporated and returns to the atmosphere, some part of it infiltrates the soil and moves downward into the groundwater system, and some part is intercepted by depressions and vegetation. The remaining amount of water on the surface of the earth, which eventually flows into streams, is called runoff.

Runoff = Precipitation - Infiltration - Interception - Evaporation

Evaporation tends to be the least of these quantities; particularly over short periods of time, and thus precipitation, infiltration, and interception are the most important variable parameters that determine runoff and eventual discharge into streams.

1. **Rainfall distribution** - If rainfall is above normal in a particular

area and infiltration, interception, and evaporation amounts are low then the resulting runoff can be high and the probability of flooding will increase. Heavy rainfall can be depicted on maps, called isohyetal maps that show curves of equal rainfall called isohyets.

2. **Lag Time** - The time difference between when heavy precipitation occurs and when peak discharge occurs in the streams draining an area is called lag time (Figure 5.3). Lag time depends on such factors as the amount of time over which the rain falls and the amount of infiltration and interception that takes place along the path to a stream. If the amount of rain is high over a short time period, shorter is the lag time and if the amount of rain is high over a longer time period, longer is the lag time. Obviously, the lack of infiltration and interception reduce lag time.

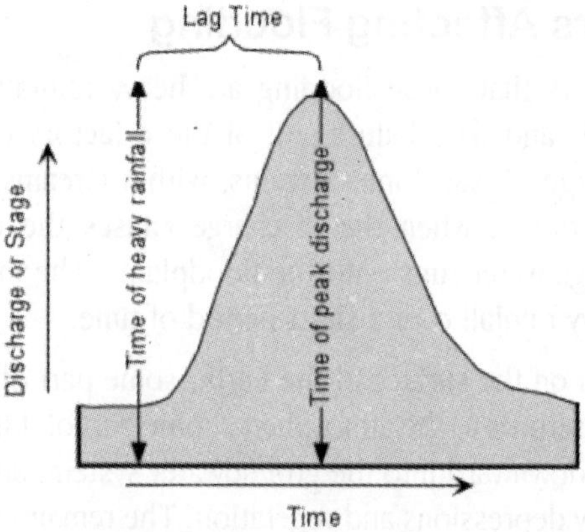

Figure 5.3 Lag time

3. **Upstream flooding**- In areas where large amounts of rain fall over a short period of time within a small area, streams in the local area may flood, with little or no effect on areas downstream known as upstream floods. In such floods, water rises quickly and flows away quickly after the storm has passed and the lag times are measured in days.

4. **Flash floods** occur when the infiltration rate is low and heavy rains occur over a short period of time. They are upstream floods with

very little lag time, may be of only a few hours. Because they come with little warning, flash floods are considered the most dangerous to human lives.

5. **Downstream flooding** - If large amounts of rain fall over an extended period of time over a large region, downstream floods may occur. Unlike upstream flooding, the lag times are usually longer as tributary streams continually increase the discharge into larger streams. Such floods extend over long periods of time and affect the larger streams as well as tributary streams. Water levels rise slowly and dissipate slowly .The 1993 flood on the upper Mississippi River is considered a downstream flood and the increase in discharge to the peak occurred over several weeks after several weeks of intense rainfall, and it took several months for river stages to return to normal levels.

6. **Infiltration** - Infiltration amount is affected by how readily the water can seep into the soil, be absorbed by the soil, and work its way down to the water table.

7. **Water saturation of the soil** - If the soil is already saturated with water and the water table has risen as a result of rainfall prior to a heavy storm, then little further water can infiltrate the soil, and the rate of infiltration will be highly decreased.

8. **Vegetation cover** - The presence of vegetation cover can increase the amount of infiltration by slowing the flow of water over the surface and providing passageways along root systems for water to enter the soil. In desert regions or deforested areas (either by fires or humans) infiltration will be reduced, thus increasing the rate of runoff and reducing the lag time.

9. **Soil types** - Different soil types have different moisture absorbing capacity. Soil type is to a large extent is influenced by the climatic conditions. For example, a type of soil that forms in dry, desert-like environments has a thin layer of poorly developed soil overlying a crust of caliche. Caliche is calcium carbonate that has precipitated out of water infiltrating though the thin soil. The caliche zone acts as an impermeable layer though which water can only penetrate with

difficulty. Such soils in deserts, in combination with sparse vegetation make flash flooding common.

10. **Frozen ground**-If the ground is frozen little water can penetrate. Thus, rainfall after a period of cold temperatures may not be able to infiltrate through the frozen ground.

11. **Human construction** - Construction activities tend to pave the surface of the earth with such things as parking lots, highways, sidewalks, and plazas that prevent infiltration of water into the soil. Furthermore, they tend to channel the water into storm sewer systems and concrete lined drainages, all of which increase runoff and decrease infiltration.

12. **Levee Failures**- As a result of flooding, natural levees are created which are relatively low and do not offer much protection from large discharge because they can easily be over topped. Human constructed levees, such as we see on the Mississippi River along much of its length, are much higher and are constructed to prevent flooding from high discharges on the River. The artificial levees are constructed of piles of rock and soil with a concrete cover on the riverside of the levee. Such levees often give a false sense of security for those living on the floodplain as the levee was built to protect, because failure of such levees can lead to flooding, either because discharge can become great enough to overtop the levees or the levees can become weakened and fail. Levees can fail due to:

a) **Over topping of levees** - If high discharge in the river leads to a river stage that is higher than any point on a levee, the water will over top the levee and start to flow onto the floodplain. Because the initial gradient from the river to flood plain is relatively high, the velocity of the stream as it over tops the levee will be high. High velocities can result in high rates of erosion, and thus the levee that is initially over topped will soon become eroded and a channel through the levee will soon be created.

b) **Undercutting and slumping of levee** - Higher discharge in the river will lead to higher velocities with the stream trying to increase its width and depth. Higher velocities can lead to higher rates of erosion along the inner parts of levees and thus lead to undercutting and slumping of the levee into the river. Heavy rainfall or seepage into the levee from the river can increase fluid pressure in the levee and lead to slumping on the outer parts of the levee. If the slumps grow to the top of the levee, large sections of the levee may slump onto the floodplain and lower the elevation of the top of the levee, allowing it to be more easily over topped.

c) **Build up of fluid pressure beneath levees** -Increasing levels of water in the river will cause the water table in the levee to rise. This will also increase fluid pressure and may result in water being pushed through the levee to rise as springs on the surrounding flood plains. If a high rate of flow is developed due to the increased fluid pressures, then a high velocity pathway to the flood plain may develop and undermine the levee causing its collapse and failure.

5.4 Floods and Their Associated Hazards

Hazards associated with flooding can be primary hazards that occur due to direct contact with water, secondary effects that occur because of the flooding, such as disruption of services, health impacts such as famine and disease or tertiary effects such as changes in the position of river channels. Major floods in China, for example, killed about 2 million people in 1887, nearly 4 million in 1931, and about 1 million in 1938. The 1993 flood on the upper Mississippi River and Midwest killed only 47 people, but the U.S. Army Corps of Engineers estimates the total economic loss at between 15 and 20 billion dollars.

1. Primary Effects

The primary effects of floods are those due to direct contact with the floodwaters. Water velocities tend to be high in floods. As discharge increases velocity increases.

- With higher velocities, streams are able to transport larger particles as suspended load. Such large particles include not only rocks and sediment, but, during a flood, could include such large objects as automobiles, houses and bridges.

• Massive amounts of erosion can be accomplished by floodwaters. Such erosion can undermine bridge structures, levees, and buildings causing their collapse.

• Water entering human built structures cause water damage. Even with minor flooding of homes, furniture is ruined, floors and walls are damaged. Automobiles affected by flooding usually results in damage that cannot easily be repaired.

• The high velocity of floodwaters allows the water to carry more sediment as suspended load. When the flood waters retreat, velocity is generally much lower and sediment is deposited. After retreat of the floodwaters everything is usually covered with a thick layer of stream deposited mud, including the interior of buildings.

• Flooding of farmland usually results in crop damage. Livestock, pets, and other animals are often carried away and drowned.

• Humans, when caught in the high velocity floodwaters, are often drowned by the water.

Floodwaters can concentrate garbage, debris, and toxic pollutants that can cause the secondary effects of health hazards.

2. Secondary and Tertiary Effects

Secondary effects are those that occur because of the primary effects and tertiary effects are the long-term changes that take place. Among the secondary effects of a flood are:

a) Secondary effects

• Drinking water supplies can get polluted if sewerage treatment plants are flooded, which may result in disease and other health effects, especially in under developed countries.

• Gas and electrical service may be disrupted.

• Transportation systems may be disrupted causing shortages of food and clean-up supplies. In under developed countries food shortages often lead to starvation.

b) Tertiary effects

- As a result of flooding, shifting of river channels may occur; new channels develop, leaving the old channels dry.

- Sediment deposited due to flooding may destroy agricultural land, although silt deposited by floodwaters could also help to increase agricultural productivity.

- Changes in ecology of the area.

5.5 Flood Control Measures

Flood control measures can be in the form of levees (both natural and man-made), floodgates, dams, and reservoirs, all constructed and designed to minimize the occurrence and/or intensity of a flood. A number of methods are used to reduce flood flows and to minimize the effects of floods.

- Flood ways are areas on the floodplain where no new structures or homes or any kind of development are allowed. Examples include green way corridors, parks, and even golf courses. Floodwalls are reinforced concrete structures parallel to riverbanks that prevent water from entering further into the floodplain.

- Dams act like a large valve regulating the rate of stream flow. A dam whose only purpose is flood control is called a flood impoundments dam. The released water flows over a spillway. However, dams also trap sediment in the reservoir that occasionally needs to be dredged out. Also, dams tend to reduce the sediment needed elsewhere, such as beaches, causing a reduction in beach area.

- Natural levees are created when rivers deposit ridges of sediment along their banks during flood events. Urbanization may remove these levees, and must be replaced artificially by earth embankments or concrete caps over an earthen core. While levees prevent flooding, they also prevent the natural fertilization from floods and also incur a false sense of security. For example, the city of New Orleans is one the largest city dependent on levees and a flood control system because the entire city is now below sea level. Massive pumping is needed during heavy rains, and the city is prone to flooding from both the Mississippi River and from the ocean. To counteract these forces, the Army Corps of Engineers has constructed a series of artificial levees that parallel the Mississippi River. Massive gates in some of the levees remain open for traffic but are closed when floods threaten. A huge spillway exists before the river reaches New Orleans that can be opened in case of flooding. Water bursting through a levee has a higher velocity, and will cause extensive damage to areas in front of the levee, sometimes even worse damage than would have resulted from the actual floodwaters. Sometimes, levees are destroyed upstream to protect areas downstream.

• Channelisation is an engineering modification of a stream channel by straightening, clearing, deepening, or lining with concrete or boulders. However, this method creates many undesirable effects like increased velocity of stream flow, removal of vegetation and the disturbance of the ecological balance.

5.6 Paleofloods

Abundant evidence can be found that provides information on how often a river floods to study the past floods. Physical evidences like stranded debris such as logs caught in a tree, ripple marks in sand above the current river level, lines of driftwood that parallel the river, trees above the current river level that are bent downstream or erosional surfaces such as scour holes above the current river level. Biologic clues like certain tree species grow only in areas that are periodically flooded. Geologic record like coarse-grained sand and larger particles such as gravel may be deposited during a flood across the floodplain. Sometimes layers of organic material left by floods can be dated using the radiocarbon dating method. This provides information on floods from hundreds, even, thousands, of years ago.

5.7 Prediction of Floods

Floods can be such devastating disasters that anyone can be affected at almost any time. When water falls on the surface of the Earth, it has to go somewhere. In order to reduce the risk due to floods, three main approaches are taken for flood prediction. Statistical studies can be undertaken to attempt to determine the probability and frequency of high discharges of streams that cause flooding. Floods can be modelled and maps can be made to determine the extent of possible flooding when it occurs in the future. And, since the main causes of flooding are abnormal amounts of rainfall and sudden thawing of snow or ice, storms and snow levels can be monitored to provide short-term flood prediction.

1. Flood hazard mapping

This is used to determine the areas susceptible to flooding when discharge of a stream exceeds the bank-full stage. Using historical data on river stages and discharge of previous floods, along with topographic data, maps can be constructed to show areas expected to be covered with floodwaters for various discharges or stages. Previous flood information for a river can be compiled to create a graph that plots discharge for varying recurrence intervals. From this graph, we obtain information on 5, 10, 20, 50, and 100-year floods. Surveys of flood-prone areas can help provide a flood hazard map for an area, which can help in the prediction of floods.

2. Monitoring the Progress of Storms

If the parameters such as amount of rainfall, degree of ground saturation, permeability of soil, and amount of vegetation can be determined, then these can be correlated to give short-term prediction, i.e. forecast of possible floods. If a forecast is issued, then a flood warning can be communicated to warn the public about the possible extent of the flood, and to give people time to move out of the area. Such forecasts are very useful for flooding that has a long lag time between the storm and the peak discharge. Flash floods, which characteristically have short lag times, are most challenging to tackle. Thus, in some areas known to be susceptible to flash floods, a flash flood warning is often issued any time heavy rainfall is expected because there is always the chance of a flash food accompanying heavy rainfall.

3. **Human Intervention**

Any alteration of the landscape has the potential consequences to cause changes in the drainage system. Sometimes attempt to modify drainage systems to prevent flooding, but these efforts can have adverse effects and actually help to cause flooding in other areas.

4. **Channel Modifications**

Engineering modifications are done such that a stream flow is controlled along a specified path for variety of reasons as flood control, enhancement of drainage, control of erosion, increasing access to the floodplain for development, or improvement of the appearance of the channel. These modifications are referred to as channelization. In order to control floods, channel modification should increase the channel cross-sectional area, so that higher discharge will not increase the stage of the river. Straighter channels also allow higher velocity flow and, enable the stream to drain faster when discharge increases. Lining the channel with concrete provides a smoother surface over which the water can flow, thereby reducing friction and also increasing the velocity of the stream. While channelization for flood control may reduce the incidence of flooding in the channelized area, it often results in more severe flooding both upstream and downstream from the channelized area.

5. **Effects of Development on Flood Hazard**

Modifications of the landscape in any way will lead to changes in the way water drains from the land. Unless careful consideration is given to the possible drainage consequences, such landscape modifications can result in higher incidence of flooding. Planning and development on the floodplains should therefore be undertaken only with great care, while the existing developments that have enhanced flooding problems are often costly and difficult to fix. Among the factors that enhance the flood potential are:

I. **Channelisation** - Most channelisation is undertaken to reduce flood hazards. But, channelisation is also undertaken to allow development on the floodplain. If the channelisation results in reducing the cross-sectional area of the stream, then the same discharge that may not have produced flooding prior to channelisation, may overflow the banks and cause extensive flooding after channelisation.

2. **Subsidence** - Subsidence often results in developed areas due to compaction of the sediment, both due to the increasing weight of structures and hydro compaction associated with the lowering of the water table. If the elevation of an area is lowered it increases the collection of more water, and in severe cases, could drastically change the drainage pattern.

3. **Storm Sewers** - In order to collect run off from streets, parking lots, and buildings, all of which block the infiltration of water into the soil, storm sewers are installed to provide underground drainage of the surface. While this may prevent local flooding of streets, it moves water more rapidly to the major stream systems and thus decreases the lag time and increases the peak discharge of the streams collecting the runoff from the storm sewers.

4. **Reduction of infiltration** – When the surface of the earth is covered with impermeable materials like concrete, asphalt, or buildings, the infiltration of water into the soil is prevented. Urbanization reduces infiltration, and thus water must collect in storm sewers and eventually in the main drainage systems. Thus, extensive urbanization also decreases the lag time and increases the peak discharge even further. Urbanization can therefore lead to a higher incidence of flash floods.

5.8 Response to Flood Hazards

Response to flood hazards can be either an engineering one (to control flooding) or a regulatory one (designed to decrease vulnerability to flooding).

I. **Engineering Approaches**

- **Channel modifications** - Channelization widens the cross-sectional area and thus creating a situation where a higher stage is necessary before flooding. In other words, by enlarging the cross-sectional area, higher discharge can be held within the channel. Channelization also increases water velocity, and thus reduces drainage time.

- **Dams** - Dams can be used to hold water back so that discharge downstream can be regulated at a desired rate. Constructed artificial dams have spillways that can be opened to reduce the level of water in the reservoir behind the dam. Thus, the water level can be lowered prior to a heavy rain, and more water can be trapped in the reservoir and released later at a controlled discharge.

- **Retention ponds** - Retention ponds serve a similar purpose to dams. Water can be trapped in a retention pond and then released at a controlled discharge to prevent flooding downstream.

- **Levees, Dikes, and Floodwalls** - These are structures built alongside the channel to increase the stage at which the stream floods.

- **Floodways** - Floodways are areas that can be built to provide an outlet to a stream and allow it flood into an area that has been designated as a floodway. Floodways are areas where no construction is allowed, and where the land is used for agricultural or recreational purposes when there is no threat of a flood, but which provide an outlet for flood waters during periods of high discharge.

2. Some non-structural measures to reduce vulnerability

With a better understanding of the stream behaviour, the probability of flooding, and areas likely to be flooded during high discharge, humans can undertake some measures to reduce vulnerability to flooding, like:

- Floodplain zoning - Laws that restrict construction and habitation of floodplains can be framed. Instead floodplains can be zoned for agricultural use, recreation, or other uses wherein lives and property are not endangered when floodwaters re-occupy the floodplain.

- Floodplain building codes - Structures that are allowed within the floodplain could be restricted those that can withstand the high velocity of flood waters and are high enough off the ground to reduce risk of contact with water.

- Floodplain buyout programs - In areas, that have been recently flooded, it may be more cost effective for the government, which usually pays for flood damage either through subsidized flood insurance or direct disaster relief, to buy the rights to the land rather than pay the cost of reconstruction and then have to pay again the next time the river floods.

• Mortgage limitations - Lending institutions could refuse to give loans to buy or construct dwellings or businesses in flood-prone areas.

Case Studies of Floods

Bangladesh - A land prone to floods

Bangladesh, a very low-lying country, is built over the flood plains of the Brahmaputra, Meghna, Ganges and Wang Rivers. The first three out of these four converge into Bangladesh, creating the largest river delta in the world and drain into the Bay of Bengal. The rise in sea water levels, the narrow north tip to the Bay of Bengal, tropical storms that whip up wind speeds of up 225 km/h, send waves (up to 26 feet tall) crashing into the coast, the shallow sea bed, the fact that water coming down from the rivers Ganges and Brahmaputra cannot escape when the water level rises and the monsoons, all contribute to the severe flooding of the Bangladesh coastline. Excessive flooding is considered a natural disaster and major flooding events recorded in recent years occurred in: 1987, 1988 and 1998. The most recent one occurred in 2007 and caused about 298 deaths, a total of 10,211,780 were affected and 58,866 houses were completely damaged by the floods. Dozens of villages were inundated when rain pushed the rivers of northwestern Bangladesh over their banks in early October 2005. To further compound the risk of flooding, Bangladesh faces frequent cyclones. Strong winds create chaos in the water, and often destroy banks and dams. Since Bangladesh is adjacent to a warm ocean, cyclones are a common occurrence. The population density on the flood plains is so great due to the fertility of the soil that many people are forced to farm on the slopes. The deforestation and agricultural practices loosen the soil, causing it to flow into the rivers when it rains resulting in the decrease of the depth of the riverbed, which increases the flooding.

Even one metre rise in ocean level can put 1/5th of Bangladesh under water and 12% of its farmland will be destroyed.

Bihar floods in 2008 caused shifting of Kosi River by 100 kms

On 18th August 2008, due to preceding heavy monsoon rains, a breach occurred in the embankments of the Kosi River, north of a dam in Nepal. About 1, 29,800-cusec water was discharged through the breach inundating hundreds of villages in north Bihar districts of Supaul, Araria, Madhepura and Purnea. The flood submerged most of the Kosi alluvial fan area, which is very fertile and has dense agrarian population. The breach caused heavy loss of life and property in the south east terai region of Nepal and in six districts of north Bihar, affecting more than 2.5 million human lives and killing about 434 people. The 2008 Bihar floods is believed to be one of the worst floods in the history of Bihar. Kosi River flows north to south, from Himalayas in Nepal and Tibet to Ganges in Bihar state of India. Usually due to heavy silt deposition, the river keeps taking longer curvilinear paths to drain into Ganges. Due to this, the river had shifted its course in the last 300 years. After the breach, the river has shifted its course nearly 100 kilometres eastward from its earlier course (which used to pass through the districts of Supaul, Saharsa, Madhubani, Darbhanga and Khagaria) and inundated areas, which had not experienced floods in the last many decades.

The 2005 Maharashtra floods: Role of funds

Severe flooding occurred in many parts of Maharashtra including large areas of the metropolis Mumbai, in which at least 1,000 people died and were caused by the eighth heaviest ever recorded 24-hour rainfall of 994 mm which lashed the city on 26th July 2005 along with torrential rainfalls which continued for the next week. The other places severely affected were Raigad, Chiplun, Ratnagiri and Kalyan in Maharashtra and the southern state of Goa. As a result of flooding which followed without warning, thousands of school children were stranded due to flooding and could not reach home for up to 18 hours and the subsequent two days were declared as school and college holidays by the state government. The Meteorological department failed to issue warnings because it lacked sophisticated weather radars, which would have given a 3-hour prior warning. The rainwater caused the sewage system to overflow causing contamination of water supply and the Government ordered all housing societies to add chlorine to their water tanks. Thousands of animal carcasses floated in the floodwaters, raising concerns about the possibility of diseases. On 11th August, the state government declared an epidemic of leptospirosis in Mumbai and its outskirts; later clarifying that there was no such threat anywhere else in Maharashtra. 66 people died of fever suspected to be leptospirosis. The financial cost of floods was about Rs 450 crore and these floods caused a stoppage of entire commercial, trading, and industrial activity for days. The secondary impacts of the floods were manifested in a variety of ways like air and rail services were disrupted. The present storm-water drainage system in Mumbai was put in place in the early 20th century and is capable of carrying only 25 millimetres of water per hour, which was extremely inadequate on a day when 994 mm of rain fell in the city. The drainage system is also clogged at several places. Only three 'outfalls' (ways out to the sea) are equipped with floodgates whereas the remaining 102 open directly into the sea. As a result, there is no way to stop the seawater from rushing into the drainage system during high tide. It was planned in 1990 to overhaul the city's storm water drainage system which had not been reviewed in over 50 years costing approximately 600 crore rupees, as proposed by UK based consultants (hired by the Brihatmumbai Municipal Corporation to study the matter). Had the project been implemented, the rainwater would not have flooded the streets of Mumbai as it would have doubled the storm water carrying capacity to 50 mm per hour. Unfortunately, the BMC committee had rejected the proposed project, as it was not feasible due to high costs involved.

Natural Service Functions of Floods:

Flooding, when viewed from the geological perspective of natural systems are not only normal, they are also essential for survival. Flooding makes soil more fertile and providing nutrients in which it is deficient. They contribute to the health of wetlands. Allowing rivers and streams to overflow their banks naturally can prevent more serious flooding downstream. Floods can distribute large amounts of water and suspended river sediment over vast areas. Floods play an important role in the functioning of ecosystems. For example, floods inundate wetland areas, creating critically important spawning and nursery sites for numerous fish species. The viability for hydrological based renewable sources of energy is higher in flood prone regions.

When floods occur

⇛Listen to the radio, television and Internet for warnings and useful information.

⇛In case of flash floods, move immediately to higher ground level.

⇛Be aware of streams, drainage channels, canyons, and other areas known to flood suddenly.

⇛Disconnect electrical appliances and keep away from electrical points.

⇛Do not walk through moving water.

⇛Do not drive into flooded areas.

Questions

Q 1. What are the causes of flooding?

Q 2. Discuss some flood control measures.

Q 3. What are the factors that affect flooding?

Q 4. Discuss the effects of flooding.

Q 5. Can floods be predicted? Discuss.

Q 6. What steps can be taken to reduce vulnerability to floods?

Some Interesting Facts

- Floods are known to cause more annual property damage than all other natural disasters combined.
- Most reptiles are unaffected by floods, but many fish die because of them.
- Floods affect and accelerate pollution levels in the river.
- About 6 inches of rapidly moving flood water can knock a person down.
- A mere 2 feet of water can float a large vehicle.
- One-third of flooded roads and bridges are so damaged by water that any vehicle trying to cross stands only a 50% chance of making it to the other side.
- Flash floods often have a dangerous wall of roaring water that carries rocks, mud, and other debris and can sweep away most things in its path.
- London is protected from flooding by a huge mechanical barrier across the River Thames, which is raised when the water level reaches a certain point
- Most deaths caused by floods are due to flash floods.

Unit 6

LANDSLIDES

'Landslides happen when small stones start to move.'

David Alton

The down slope movement of small stones, soil and rock fragments, even if very slow should not be underestimated as these processes can ultimately result in landslide hazards. Downward movement of slope-forming materials like rock, soil, artificial fill, or a combination of these can result in landslide. These materials can move by falling, toppling, sliding, spreading, or flowing. Landslides or mass wasting is the down-slope movement of regolith (loose uncemented mixture of soil and rock particles that covers the Earth's surface) due to gravity without the help of geological agents such as water, ice, or wind. Contributory factors include soil saturation from rainfall or seepage, or human activity (i.e. vegetation removal, construction of roads, railways or buildings on steep terrain) or in some cases natural hazards like earthquakes, volcanoes. Landslides are downslope displacements of regolith, rock, and soil. Because landslides are more than simply "slides" and can also occur under the sea, it is better to term them as mass movements. Mass movements are one of the most serious threats in areas with steep slopes. Mass-wasting is part of a continuum of erosional processes between weathering and stream transport. Mass-wasting causes regolith to move down-slope where sooner or later the loose particles will be picked up by another geological agent and eventually moved to a site of deposition such as an ocean basin or a lake bed. In order for regolith to move in a mass wasting process it must be on a slope, since gravity will only cause motion if the material is on a slope.

6.1 Factors Causing Landslides

When the slope stability changes from a stable to an unstable condition, landslides occur. A change in the stability of a slope can be caused by a number of factors, acting together or alone and can be due to natural or anthropogenic reasons.

Natural causes include:

- Pressure of groundwater can destabilize the slope
- Absence or loss of vertical vegetative structure, soil nutrients/ structure
- Erosion of the top of a slope by rivers or ocean waves
- Weakening of a slope through saturation by snowmelt, glaciers melting, or heavy rains
- Earthquakes adding loads to barely-stable slopes or earthquake-caused liquefaction destabilizing slopes volcanic eruptions

Human or Anthropogenic causes include:

- Vibrations from machinery or traffic
- Blasting or mining activity
- Earthwork which alters the shape of a slope, or which imposes new loads on an existing slope
- In shallow soils, the removal of deep-rooted vegetation that binds colluviums to bedrock
- Construction, agricultural, or forestry activities which change the amount of water which infiltrates into the soil

6.2 Failure of Slope

Slope failures are recognized as a significant natural hazard. Slope failure can be defined as a downward movement of a large amount of material. They can occur suddenly in one easily recognized movement, or may occur almost imperceptibly over a long period of several years. A slope failure is classified based on how it moves and the type of material being moved. Slope failures cause damage to highways, homes, and other property. Slope failures can be due to natural events like earthquakes, heavy rainfall from thunderstorms, volcanic eruptions, flooding, or even freezing and thawing of soil moisture. Several events and scientific studies have confirmed that almost any modification of a slope by people increases the risk of slope movement, especially in areas already susceptible to these natural hazards.

6.3 Factors Leading to Slope Failures

Mountainous regions, hilly regions, and coastlines have the largest reports of slope failures. Also, tectonically active regions are prone to slope failures triggered by earthquakes or volcanic activity. Sinkholes are a common geological feature in karst landscapes, where water has dissolved underlying bedrock, typically limestone or gypsum, causing subsidence and slope failures. Slope failures can occur in any season and there is more probability in certain seasons if they are triggered by weather events such as rain, snow, or freezing and thawing of soil water. Streams eroding their banks or surf action along a coast can undercut a slope making it unstable (Figure 6.1).

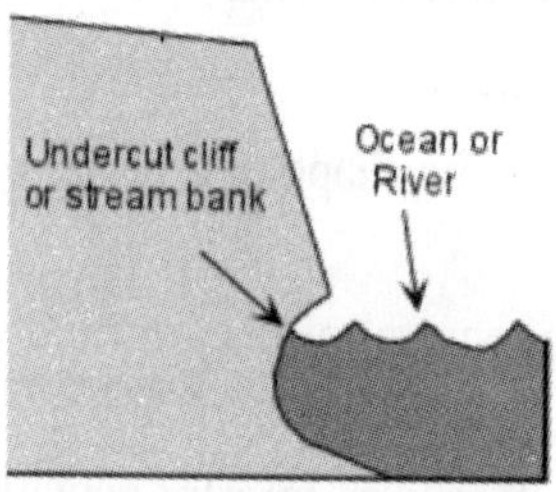

Figure 6.1 Undercutting - streams eroding their banks or surf action along a coast can undercut a slope making it unstable

Slope failures can occur nearly everywhere where slopes exist and it can be triggered by weather conditions, geologic events, human modification of the landscape, or most commonly, some interaction of all of the above (Figure 6.2).

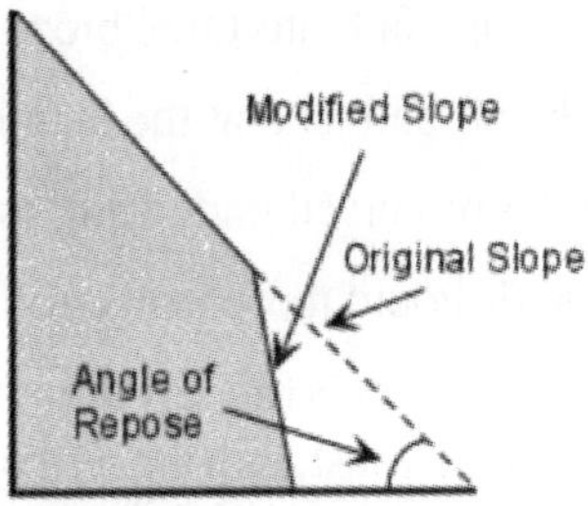

Figure 6.2 Unstable slope due to slope modification

6.4 Different Kinds of Mass Movements

The landslides can be differentiated by the different kinds of material involved and the mode of movement. A classification system based on these parameters is given below.

Table 6.1 Types of landslides. Abbreviated version of Varnes' classification of slope movements (Varnes, 1978)

Type of Landslide	Type of Material		
	Bedrock	Soils	
		Predominantly Coarse	Predominantly Fine
A. FALLS	Rock fall	Debris fall	Earth fall
B. TOPPLES	Rock topple	Debris slide	Earth slide
C. SLIDES ROTATIONAL	Rock slide	Debris slide	Earth slide
TRANSLATIONAL			
D. LATERAL SPREADS	Rock spread	Debris spread	Earth spread
E. FLOWS	Rock flow(deep creep)	Debris flow	Earth flow
		(Soil creep)	
F. COMPLEX	Combination of two or more principal types of movement		

Mass movements down slope fall into three broad categories:

- Falls move through the air and land at the base of a slope
- Slides move along a flat or curved underlying surface
- Flows occur as plastic or liquid movements from water saturation

The speed of these mass movements can vary from very slow movements unnoticed for years to extremely fast, moving well over a hundred miles per hour.

The fall of a rock particle through the air from a cliff is called a rock fall (Figure 6.3). Though Earthquakes can trigger rock fall events, frost wedging is the common cause. Unlike rock fall, flows are mass movements in which the material acts like a liquid or fluid, and occur in a wide variety of speeds.

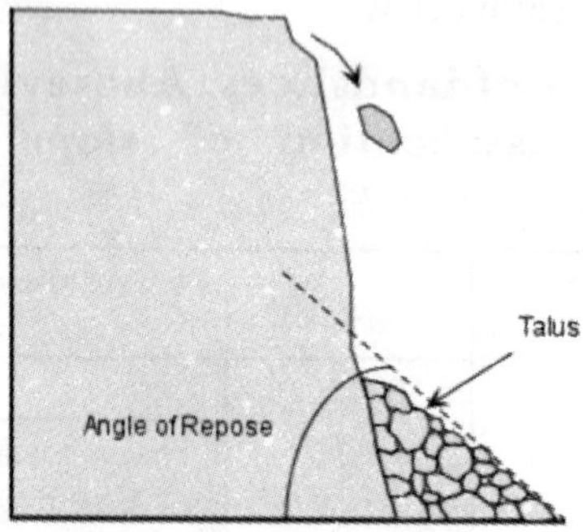

Figure 6.3 Rock and debris fall

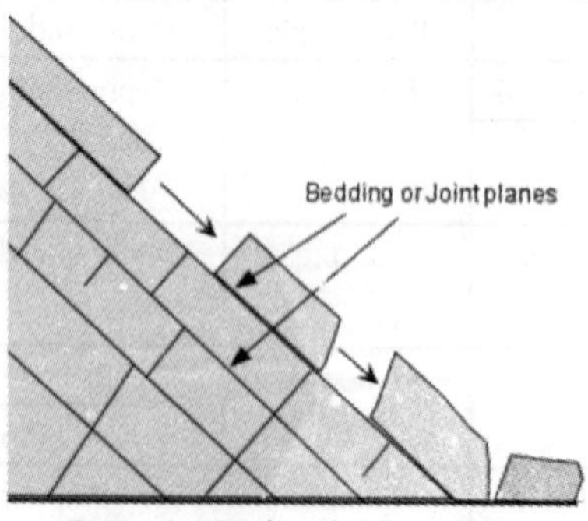

Figure 6.4 Rock and debris slides

Slides occur along flat or curved underground surfaces. Rock slides occur along a flat surface, usually when the layers of underlying rock are tilted at an angle, and are especially hazardous along road cuts (Figure 6.4).

Creep is the very slow down slope displacement of soil and regolith. Creep occurs on slopes when frost lifts the soil and then places it further downslope. Gravity also acts to pull the upper layers of soil and regolith downslope, causing fences, telephone poles to be tilted.

Slumps occur when material slides along a curved surface. Slumping is caused by erosion at the base of the slope, perhaps by water action, a common coastal hazard. Slumping can also occur when excessive water is added to a slope (Figure 6.5). The steep slope at the head of the slump is called a scarp.

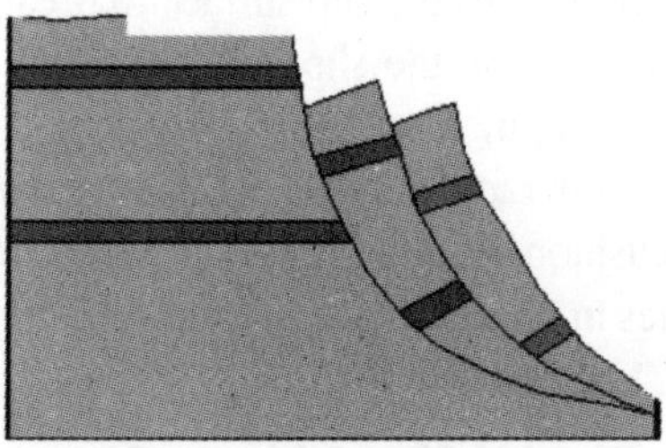

Figure 6.5 Slump

Solifluction occurs when the upper layers of soil become saturated and move downslope, common in very cold climates where permafrost forms. During the summer, the upper layer of the permafrost melts, saturating the ground and causing solifluction lobes. Mudflows are mixtures of water and soil (up to 30% water) and occur where water has saturated the soil to the point the soil becomes a liquid. They occur after forest fires have denuded the vegetation, and also occur around construction sites.

A debris flow is a very rapid down slope movement of rock debris and regolith. They often start as slumps or slides, but become debris flows as the material mixes with more water and even air. Debris flows gain their rapid speed because they actually ride on a cushion of air as they flow down slope as confirmed by experimental observations. A debris avalanche is an extremely rapid downward movement of rock debris, regolith, and soil, more common in areas with steep slopes. The term avalanche is generally applied to any type of fast-moving downward movement of any type of material, but is associated with much steeper slopes than debris flows. Such debris avalanches move down slope through avalanche chutes. Major hazards occur when large masses of snow break loose and flow like a liquid called snow avalanches. Every year, several deaths are reported in the US and in Europe due to the snow avalanches. As snow becomes compacted, it actually releases a little heat due to high pressure and the snow becomes granular. Those intermediate layers of snow, called a slip surface, are much more prone to slippage than the overlying layers of snow. An avalanche occurs when the accumulated snow causes the slip surface to break. Avalanches also occur when vibrations cause the slip surface to fail and these can be caused by an earthquake, by noise from snow cannon, by skiers, and by snowmobiles. The snow rapidly mixed with air as it moves downslope, again creating a cushion that increases the speed of the avalanche. Anything that comes in its path, such as trees, buildings, cars on roads, towns and people, is destroyed.

6.5 Factors That Affect Mass Movement

- **Rate of Land Movement** - This varies from exceptionally slow, only a few centimetres per year (which can damage roads, buildings, pipelines, etc) to a sudden total collapse or avalanche of perhaps millions of tones of debris, with the potential to crush vehicles, buildings and people, or to sweep away roads, power and telephone lines.

- **Degree of Land Movement** - The distance travelled by landslide debris can also vary greatly, from a few centimetres in 'ground slumps', to many kilometres when large mudflows follow river valleys.

Two types of forces combine in any type of mass movement: driving forces that promote movement, and resisting forces that deter movement. Whenever the driving forces are greater than the resisting forces, the material on the slope breaks loose and moves down slope.

A. Driving Forces:

i) **Gravity** - Steeper the slope, the greater is the tendency of materials to move down slope. Gravity is the primary driving force and can be influenced by human activity, such as excavation. When a portion of a slope moves downward as a result of either natural conditions or human activity, this process is known as slope failure.

ii) **Rock Structure** – Rock structure can be an important driving force as rocks are far from being completely solid and most have pore spaces, which allow water and air to infiltrate. Rocks can break along natural fractures and joints in the rock caused by stress and the contact surfaces between different rock types are the planes of weakness. In all highway and building construction, engineering geologists conduct studies to determine the stability of the slopes when building highways, railways, canals, and any type of construction site. Plate tectonic movements may cause rock layers to become tilted, which can become unstable if they're tilted in the same direction as the slope itself.

iii) **Water** - Water is an important driving force, but its role is complex, because it can also act as resisting force in certain circumstances. Water increases the weight of slope material by filling previously empty pores and fractures and promotes mass movement. For example, a sandy slope can have up to 35% pore space. After a prolonged period of rain, the pores may be completely filled, increasing the weight of the sediment, which will increase the probability for movement by gravity. Water can decrease the strength of the rock or sediment by reducing cohesion among the particles. For example, water circulating in limestone can dissolve the calcium carbonate particles, reducing cohesion of the rock. Water can also infiltrate pore space, then freeze (frost heaving), breaking the rock apart. Water can create shrink-swell clays, which are a common hazard in the construction of building foundations. In clay-rich sediments, clay-sized particles attract and absorb water molecules, causing the sediment to swell to many times its original volume. The best known of these clays is bentonite. Between rains, these clay-rich sediments can shrink and contract, forming large surface cracks that can damage any structures built on top. Finally, clays can be turned to liquid in a process called liquefaction. Quick clay is formed by this process, and can occur when saltwater ions, which normally help to hold the sediment together, are flushed out and replaced with freshwater. Solid clay-rich sediment transforms to very unstable quick clay.

B. Resisting Forces

Water can also act as a resisting force to mass movement in certain cases. In sediment pore spaces that are not completely filled, the thin film of water actually makes the particles stick together due to cohesion. Cohesion is the ability of particles to attract and hold each other together. Water molecules that line the pore spaces tend to hold other molecules - this attraction is called surface tension, a force that holds water together. The complex role of water can be appreciated by taking the sand castle as an example. Without water, it is impossible to build a sand castle. With just the right amount of water, one can build a sand castle because the water creates surface tension that holds particles together. When the sand castle becomes saturated with high tide, the castle breaks apart, because the pore spaces have been completely filled with water, which is now a driving force.

The angle of repose is the maximum angle on a slope to which sediment particles can be piled. Some sediment can accumulate in large volumes, yet remain stable. Some factors that affect the stability of particles on a slope include:

• Particle size: larger particles maintain a steeper slope than smaller particles.

• Particle shape: particles with angular edges can have a steeper slope than ones with rounded edges

• Particle sorting: poorly sorted particles have all sizes represented. These can have steeper slopes because the smaller particles can fill the spaces between the larger particles.

• Particle moisture: particles with some water can have a steeper slope than particles with no or too much water.

Finally, particle packing will affect the ability of sediment to move down slope. Packing describes the arrangement of particles in sediment.

Cubic packing occurs when grains are aligned with their centres above one another, and represents loose sediment. Rhombohedral packing occurs when the centres of the grains of sediment are located over the spaces between the grains. This type of packing occurs in sediments that have "settled" due to shaking or sorting by water movement.

6.6 Prediction of Mass Movements

Construction activities should be careful about causing steeper slopes by undermining the base of slopes, as steeper slopes are also more prone to slippage in seismic areas. Slopes are considered unstable if they are composed of rocks that can be easily dissolved, such as limestone. Slopes are also considered unstable if the layers of rocks are tilted rather than horizontal. Slopes that are constantly waterlogged or highly saturated are considered unstable. Some clues to look for are springs along the slope, areas of soggy ground, and standing pools of water.

Some clues that indicate an old slump:

- Hummocky ground at the base of a slope
- Trees that are different in age - young trees occur in the slump itself and older trees grow outside the slump
- Fence lines may also be displaced.

Increased rates of soil creep maybe indicated by down slope tilting of trees and vegetation growing on the slope. This suggests a rapid creep rate down slope.

Geologic maps of an area can be used to help create a landslide potential map, and uses the type of rock underlying the surface, as well as the steepness of the slopes. The areas where steep slopes and weak rocks combine are designated as slide prone.

6.7 Landslides and Their Effects

- Landslides and Water - Slope saturation by water is a primary cause of landslides. This effect can occur in the form of intense rainfall, snowmelt, changes in ground-water levels, and water-level changes along coastlines, earth dams, and the banks of lakes, reservoirs, canals, and rivers.

• Landsliding and flooding are closely related because both are related to precipitation, runoff, and the saturation of ground by water and in fact these two events often occur simultaneously in the same area. Landslides can cause overtopping of reservoirs and/or reduced capacity of reservoirs to store water. In addition, debris flows and mudflows usually occur in small, steep stream channels and often are mistaken for flood. Landslides can cause flooding by forming landslide dams that block valleys and stream channels, allowing large amounts of water to back up. This causes backwater flooding and, if the dam fails, subsequent downstream flooding. Also, solid landslide debris can "bulk" or add volume and density to otherwise normal stream flow or cause channel blockages and diversions creating flood conditions or localized erosion.

• Landslides and Seismic Activity - The occurrence of earthquakes in steep landslide-prone areas greatly increases the likelihood that landslides will occur, due to ground shaking alone or shaking-caused dilation of soil materials, which allows rapid infiltration of water. Loosening of rocks as a result of ground shaking also causes widespread rock falls. The 1964 Great Alaska Earthquake caused widespread land sliding monetary loss due to the earthquake. Many mountainous areas that are vulnerable to landslides have also experienced at least moderate rates of earthquake occurrence in recorded times.

• Landslides and Volcanic Activity –Volcanic lava can melt snow at a rapid rate, causing a deluge of rock, soil, ash, and water that accelerates rapidly on the steep slopes of volcanoes, devastating anything in its path and are some of the most devastating types. These volcanic debris flows (also known as lahars) reach great distances and can damage structures in flat areas surrounding the volcanoes. The 1980 eruption of Mount St. Helens, in Washington, triggered a massive landslide on the north flank of the volcano, the largest landslide in recorded times.

• Landslide Effects on Buildings - Landslides can occur where the terrain has been altered by humans or geologically and can damage buildings. As pressures on the ground increase, so does the likelihood of buildings being devastated.

• Landslide Effects on Plant-life - Landslides can affect plant-life and ecology as any kind of plant-life in the slides way will get washed down with the slide. The steeper a slope, the more likely a slide will occur. The weaker the rock and sediments are, the more prone they become to a landslide occurring. If land becomes saturated, the land may flow more easily.

6.8 Precursor Events Before The Occurence Of Landslides

- Springs or saturated grounds that are normally wet are not so. Also, water breaks through the ground surface in new locations.
- New cracks or bulges in the ground can be a prediction to landslides.
- If concrete foundations crack or move, a landslide can perhaps occur.
- When poles, trees, or fences begin to lean, a slide may be on its way also.
- Doors or windows begin to stick together or jam
- New cracks begin to appear in plaster, tile, brick, or foundations.
- Outside walls, walk ways and/or stairs begin to pull away from the building.
- Cracks begin to widen on the ground or on paved areas such as streets.
- An underground utility line begins to break.

6.9 Prevention and Mitigation of Mass Movements

Vulnerability to landslide hazards is a function of location, type of human activity, use, and frequency of landslide events. The effects of landslides on people and structures can be reduced by total avoidance of landslide hazard areas or by restricting, prohibiting, or imposing conditions on hazard-zone activity. Landslide effects can be reduced through proper land-use planning, policies and regulations by the local governments. Individuals can reduce their exposure to hazards by educating themselves on the past hazard history of a site and by making inquiries to planning and engineering departments of local governments. They can also obtain the professional advice of geologist, who can properly evaluate the hazard potential of a site.

The hazard from landslides can be reduced by avoiding construction on steep slopes and existing landslides, or by stabilizing the slopes. Stability increases when ground water is prevented from rising in the landslide mass by (1) covering the landslide with an impermeable membrane, (2) directing surface water away from the landslide, (3) draining ground water away from the landslide, and (4) minimizing surface irrigation.

Some mitigation measures are summarized below:

1. Primarily we should avoid building in an area prone to mass movements, but this is not always possible because of increasing populations.

2. Slopes should be drained and could be achieved by:

- Interceptor drains can be built at the top of the slope to channel water away.

- Perforated pipes can be driven into the slope to capture water and drain it away by gravity.

- Wells can be driven into the slope to allow water to be pumped away.

3. Slope reduction: the steepness of the slopes can be manually decreased by construction. This is sometimes not economically feasible, so benches or terraces could be constructed.

4. Concrete coatings can be applied to the slope to seal the slope and prevent water from infiltrating, and also to prevent frost wedging. Retaining walls can be constructed at the base of slopes. Rock bolts can be drilled into tilting rock layers to prevent them from slipping.

5. Structures can be built in areas prone to mass movements. A more popular one is the use of cable nets and wire fences to catch rocks

and debris from tumbling down into highways and neighbourhoods. Intercept ditches can be built to catch any falling debris and prevent it from rolling onto a road. Rock sheds and tunnels can be built and avalanche sheds can be built in areas prone to snow avalanches.

Case Studies

Darjeeling, India: ideal conditions for tea growth but bad for slope stability

Tea plantations from Darjeeling are famous worldwide known for its unique flavour. The tea plantations require rolling topography, moderate temperatures and high rainfall conditions, which are present in Darjeeling but are bad for stable slope conditions. Proper management of the landscape, the tea plantations and contour landscaping can help control the landslides. Many Himalayan regions, including Darjeeling is currently facing a right combination of conditions that promote landslides - rapid population growth, deforestation, uncontrolled building to low standards, intense monsoon rainfall, and the construction of low cost roads with poor engineering standards. During September 2007 intense monsoon rainfall in the Kalimpong region of Darjeeling in Northern India triggered large numbers of landslides, killing about seven people. This has brought the issue of environmental degradation and the consequent landslides in Himalayan environments for much greater attention for proper landscape management.

Landslides triggered by torrential rain in Brazil

Brazil's Santa Catarina state experienced more than 4,000 landslides after months of torrential rain in November 2008. Many houses and their residents were buried in massive rivers of mud. The floods and mudslides affected up to 2 million people displacing some 100,000 people. The death toll from mudslides was around 110 with 20 others missing, while the landslide killed more than 100 and displaced 54,000 people. Blumenau was one of five towns in the Itajai valley of Santa Catarina state, to declare a state of emergency with its main river that rose by about 12 metres submerging large areas.

2007 Chittagong mudslide-cost of ignoring the experts' advice

Bangladesh's annual monsoon for 2007 started with unusually heavy rain, intensified by a storm from the Bay of Bengal on June 9-June 10, 2007. By June 11, more than one-third of the southeastern coastal city of Chittagong was under water. In addition to the floods, the rains triggered devastating landslides in the deforested hills on which the city is built. The Chittagong Mudslide occurred in the port city of Chittagong in southeastern Bangladesh. Heavy monsoon rainfall caused landslides that engulfed slums around the hilly areas of the city. Scientists had predicted the probability of landslides due to the Bangladesh government's failure in curbing the illegal hill cutting taking place in Chittagong. One-third of Chittagong, a city of five million residents, came under water due to heavy rainfall and tidal water. The flash floods in the hills caused mudslides and rubble to bury shanties at the foot of the hills near Chittagong Cantonment. The death toll was reported to be at least 128, including at least 59 children, with more than 150 injured. The government asked the local authorities to evacuate 8,000 people from Lebubagan, the worst hit area. Most of the deaths were a result of the landslides or from buildings collapsing in the rain. Communication services like telephone and radio had been disrupted.

Natural Service Functions of Landslides

Landslides are a natural process that can have some positive ecological benefits, such as renewal of supplies of large woody debris and gravels that are necessary for healthy aquatic systems. Landslides replenish soil, which sustains life.

When landslides occur

Before

⇛Before moving or occupying a building, check for the area's history of landslides or instability and do not build near steep slopes.

⇛In steep areas, look for signs of ground movement such as trees tilting (down-slope), water seepage and breaks in the ground.

During

⇛Move away from the path of a landslide or debris flow immediately or as quickly as possible.

⇛Roll into a tight ball and protect your head in case escape is not possible.

⇛If indoors, take shelter at the least-affected end of the building under a strong table or bench. If outdoors, avoid the tops and bases of cliffs, mountains and embankments, especially where there are signs of loose rocks or debris.

⇛If a landslide threatens, move quickly from its path and keep clear of banks, trees, power lines and poles.

After

⇛Stay away from steep slopes, as there could be danger of additional slides.

⇛Check for injured and trapped persons near the slide, without entering the direct slide area.

⇛Check for secondary effects like broken electrical, water, gas, and sewage lines and damaged roadways and railways.

⇛Erosion caused by loss of ground cover can lead to flash flooding and additional landslides in the near future and the affected area needs to be made stable.

Questions

1. Define landslides with suitable examples.
2. Explain the different types of mass movements?
3. Describe the factors that cause slope failures and mass movement.
4. Write short notes on (a) driving forces (b) resisting forces.
5. How can we predict mass movements?
6. What are the effects of landslides?
7. Describe the prevention and mitigation of mass movements.

Some Interesting Facts

- Approximately 25% of the world's populations live in karst landscapes.
- Landslides usually have a greater chance to occur where existing ones or recent ones have taken place.
- Landslides can even occur underwater. Submarine landslides are underwater landslides and can trigger monster tidal waves that wreck coastal regions. Earthquakes precede many underwater landslides, which then produce the colossal waves known as tsunamis.
- Venus and Mars have been subject to long-term mapping by orbiting satellites, and occurrences of landslides have been observed.
- The fast moving landslides are debris flows, mudslides, mudflows, lahars, or debris avalanches and normally occur during periods of intense rainfall or rapid snow melt.
- Every year, landslides in the United States cause approximately $3.5 billion in damage, and kill between 25 and 50 people.
- Landslides often accompany earthquakes, floods, storm surges, hurricanes, wildfires, or volcanic activity. They are often more damaging and deadly than the triggering event.
- The eruption of the Mount St. Helens volcano, May 1980 caused one of the largest landslides in history. It was a rock slide-debris avalanche large enough to fill 250 million dump trucks.

Glossary

Natural Disasters

Earth processes are the natural processes that occur within the earth i.e. lithosphere, hydrosphere or atmosphere.

Geo-hazard is a natural earth process that upon interaction with humans causes loss of life and / or property.

Hazard is a potential threat to humans and their welfare and risk as the probability of hazard occurrence, where as disaster can be defined as the realization of the hazard.

Natural disaster - is an event caused by natural forces of nature affecting human life and / or property.

Nuclear holocaust is the complete or almost complete wiping out of human civilization by nuclear warfare.

Technological hazards, unlike natural hazards, occur as a result of human interaction with the environment causing loss of human life and / or property.

Vulnerability refers to not only the possible physical effects of a natural hazard, but the way it affects human life and property.

Earthquakes

Aftershocks are smaller earthquakes, which occur after the main earthquake

Body waves are seismic waves that propagate from earthquake focus to the surface and can be either primary (P) or secondary (S) waves.

Compression Waves are the wave motion due to expansion and compression.

Elastic Rebound Model states that the sudden release of stored strain in rocks is due to movement along a fault.

Epicentre is the location on Earth's surface that lies directly above the focus of an earthquake.

Fault Scarp A steep slope or cliff formed directly by movement along a fault and representing the exposed surface of the fault before modification by erosion and weathering.

Fault is a fracture in the earth's surface.

Focus is the zone within Earth where rock displacement produces an earthquake.

Fracture is the manner of breaking due to intense folding or faulting.

Hypocentre is the location on a buried fault where an earthquake occurs.

Intensity is a measure of the effects of an earthquake at a particular place and depends not only on the magnitude of the earthquake, but also on the distance from the epicentre and the local geology.

Joint is a surface of fracture in a rock.

Lithosphere is the rigid outer layer of Earth, including the crust and upper mantle

Magnitude is the numerical expression of the amount of energy released by an earthquake, determined by measuring earthquake waves on standardized recording instruments (seismographs.) The number scale for measuring earthquake magnitudes is logarithmic rather than arithmetic.

Mantle is the zone of the earth between the crust and the core.

Mercalli intensity scale is a scale used for measuring the intensity of an earthquake.

Mid-oceanic ridge is an underwater mountain range, typically having a valley known as a rift running along its axis, formed due to plate movements. As mid-ocean ridge demarcates the boundary between two tectonic plates and the plates spread apart it is termed a divergent plate boundary.

Richter magnitude scale, or more correctly local magnitude ML scale, assigns a single number to quantify the amount of seismic energy released by an earthquake.

Ring of Fire is the region of mountain-building earthquakes and volcanoes surrounding the Pacific Ocean.

Seismic waves are waves that travel through the Earth as the result of an earthquake, explosion, or some other process that imparts forces to the body.

Seismograph is an instrument used to record seismic waves; that is, vibrations of the earth.

Seismologist: Geologists who study earthquake waves.

Seismology is the scientific study of earthquakes and the propagation of elastic waves through the Earth.

Seismometers are instruments that measure and record motions of the ground, including those of seismic waves generated by earthquakes, nuclear explosions, and other seismic sources.

Shear Waves: Earthquake waves that move up and down as the wave itself moves.

Shearing: The motion of surfaces sliding past one another.

Strike-Slip Fault: A nearly vertical fault with sideslipping displacement.

Subduction zone: A long, narrow zone where one lithospheric plate descends beneath another.

Surface waves, unlike body waves, are seismic waves that travel along the outer layer of the Earth and can be either Love or Rayleigh waves.

Theory of Plate Tectonics states that the lithosphere is divided into a number of relatively rigid lithospheric plates that collide with, separate from, and translate past one another at their boundaries.

Tremor is low amplitude, continuous earthquake activity often associated with magma movement.

Tsunami is the huge wave generated in the sea due to a submarine earthquake, volcanic eruption, or large landslide.

Volcanoes

Active Volcano: A volcano that is active, i.e. erupting.

Ash Flow: A turbulent mixture of gas and rock fragments, most of which are ash-sized particles, ejected violently from a crater or fissure.

Ash: Fine particles of pulverized rock blown from an explosion vent, measuring less than 1/10 inch in diameter and may be either solid or molten when first erupted.

Ashfall: Volcanic ash that has fallen through the air from an eruption cloud. The deposit is usually well-sorted and layered.

Avalanche is a large mass of material or mixtures of material falling or sliding rapidly under the force of gravity. Avalanches are often characterised by their content, such as snow, ice, soil, or rock avalanches. A mixture of these materials is a debris avalanche.

Basalt is a volcanic rock, dark in colour, with 45% to 54% silica, and is rich in iron and magnesium.

Block is an angular chunk of solid rock ejected during a volcanic eruption.

Bomb is a fragment of molten or semi-molten rock, which is blown out during an eruption. Because of their plastic condition, bombs are often modified in shape during their flight or upon impact.

Caldera is a volcanic crater more than 1 km in diameter, formed at the summit of a volcano when lava is drained from an underground magma chamber, causing the summit of the volcano to be unsupported, and to collapse.

Central Vent: A central vent is an opening at the earth's surface of a volcanic conduit of cylindrical or pipe-like form connecting the surface to the magma chamber.

Cinder Cone: A volcanic cone built entirely of loose fragmented material (pyroclastics.)

Composite Volcano: A steep volcanic cone built by both lava flows and pyroclastic eruptions.

Conduit: A passage followed by magma in a volcano.

Continental Crust: Solid, outer layers of the earth, in the rocks of the continents.

Continental Drift: The theory that horizontal movement of the earth's surface causes slow, relative movements of the continents toward or away from one another.

Dome: A steep-sided mass of viscous (doughy) lava extruded from a volcanic vent (often circular in plane view) and spiny, rounded, or flat on top.

Dormant Volcano is used to describe a volcano which is presently inactive but which may erupt again.

Eruption Cloud is the column of gases, ash, and larger rock fragments rising from a crater or other vent.

Eruption: The process by which solid, liquid, and gaseous materials are ejected into the earth's atmosphere and onto the earth's surface by volcanic activity.

Extinct Volcano: A volcano that is not presently active and is not likely to do so for a very long time in the future.

Fissures: Elongated fractures or cracks on the slopes of a volcano. Fissure eruptions typically produce liquid flows, but pyroclastics may also be ejected.

Flank Eruption: An eruption from the side of a volcano (in contrast to a summit eruption.)

Fumarole: A vent or opening through which issue steam, hydrogen sulphide, or other gases. The craters of many dormant volcanoes contain active fumaroles. Fumaroles are secondary vents on the flank of a volcano, which emit steam and other gases.

Hotspot: A narrow stream of hot mantle convecting up from the Earth's core-mantle boundary called a mantle plume causes hotspot. Hot-spot Volcanoes are volcanoes related to a persistent heat source in the mantle.

Intrusion: The process of emplacement of magma in pre-existing rock.

Lahar: A torrential flow of water-saturated volcanic debris down the slope of a volcano in response to gravity.

Lava Flow: An outpouring of lava onto the land surface from a vent or fissure. Also, a solidified tongue-like or sheet-like body formed by outpouring lava.

Lava: Magma, which has reached the surface through a volcanic eruption.

Magma Chamber: The subterranean cavity containing the gas-rich liquid magma, which feeds a volcano.

Magma: Molten rock beneath the surface of the earth.

Pillow lava: Interconnected, sack-like bodies of lava formed underwater.

Pipe is a vertical conduit through the Earth's crust below a volcano, through which magmatic materials have passed and is commonly filled with volcanic breccia and fragments of older rock.

Pit crater are collapse features on the flanks or summit of a volcano that are smaller than the main caldera at the summit of a volcano.

Plinian Eruption: An explosive eruption in which a steady, turbulent stream of fragmented magma and magmatic gases is released at a high velocity from a vent. Large volumes of tephra and tall eruption columns are characteristic.

Plug: Solidified lava that fills the conduit of a volcano.

Pluton is a large igneous intrusion formed at great depth in the crust.

Pyroclastic Flow: Lateral flowage of a turbulent mixture of hot gases and unsorted pyroclastic material (volcanic fragments, crystals, ash, pumice, and glass shards.

Pyroclastic refers to fragmented (clastic) rock material formed by a volcanic explosion or ejection from a volcanic vent.

Rhyolite is a volcanic rock that is light in colour, contains 69% silica or more, and is rich in potassium and sodium.

Seamount: A submarine volcano.

Shield Volcano is a gently sloping volcano in the shape of a flattened dome and built almost exclusively of lava flows.

Stratovolcano is a volcano composed of both lava flows and pyroclastic material.

Strombolian Eruption: A type of volcanic eruption characterized by jetting of clots or fountains of fluid basaltic lava from a central crater.

Surge: A ring-shaped cloud of gas and suspended solid debris that moves radially outward at high velocity as density flows from the base of a vertical eruption column accompanying a volcanic eruption or crater formation.

Tephra is the erupted material of all types and sizes from a crater or volcanic vent and deposited from the air.

Tuff is a volcanic rock formed of pyroclastic material.

Vesicle is a small air cavity formed in volcanic rock during solidification.

Volcanic Arc is a curved linear belt of volcanoes above a subduction zone.

Volcano: A vent in the surface of the Earth through which magma and associated gases and ash erupt.

Vulcan: Roman god of fire and the forge after whom volcanoes are named.

Weather-related Hazards

Acid rain - When rainwater goes below a pH of 5.6, it is called acid rain as normal rainwater has a pH of 5.6 due to the dissolution of CO_2 in rainwater.

Climate change refers to the changes in the long-term climate or changes in the average weather for a particular location and can result from natural processes, such as the change in the sun's strength, or from human activities, through the build-up of greenhouse gases.

Cyclogenesis describes the process of cyclone formation.

Desertification is a land degradation process occurring in arid, semiarid and dry sub-humid areas of the world.

Drainage Basin: The area of land drained by a river system.

Drought is an extended period of months or years when a region experiences a noticeable deficiency in its water supply consistently below average precipitations.

El Niño and La Niña – El Niño-Southern Oscillation, commonly referred to as ENSO is a global coupled ocean-atmosphere phenomenon. The two important temperature fluctuations in surface waters of the tropical Eastern Pacific Ocean are the El Niño and La Niña.

Famine refers to the complete absence of food and is manifested by malnutrition, starvation, population explosions and natural disasters.

Hail is a rain of semi-spherical, concentrically layered ice balls that are dropped from some thunderstorms.

Hurricanes are massive tropical cyclonic storms with winds exceeding 119 km/hr. It forms and intensify over tropical oceanic regions. In the Atlantic Ocean and eastern Pacific Ocean they are called hurricanes, typhoons in western Pacific, and cyclones in the southern hemisphere.

Lightning is the electrical discharge from clouds, which causes thunder.

Nor'easters are extra tropical cyclonic storms that originate outside of the tropics.

Pacific typhoon or tropical storm is a tropical cyclone that forms in the northwestern Pacific Ocean. The basin is demarcated within the Pacific Ocean from Asia, north of the equator, and west of the International Date Line.

Tornadoes are funnel-shaped clouds that are associated with thunderstorms. A tornado develops within a severe thunderstorm when there is an excessive amount of vertical wind shear.

Floods

Flood is an overflow of an expanse of water that submerges land, a deluge.

Fluvial: Produced by the action of flowing water.

Landslides

Avalanche is generally applied to any type of fast-moving downward movement of any type of material.

Creep is the very slow down slope displacement of soil and regolith.

Debris flow is a very rapid down slope movement of rock debris and regolith. They often start as slumps or slides, but become debris flows as the material mixes with more water and even air.

Flows are mass movements in which the material acts like a liquid or fluid, and occur in a wide variety of speeds.

Landslide is a mass movement phenomenon that includes a wide range of ground movement, such as rock falls, deep failure of slopes and shallow debris flows, which can occur in offshore, coastal and onshore environments.

Mudflow: A flowage of water-saturated earth material possessing a high degree of fluidity during movement.

Nuees Ardentes: A French term applied to a highly heated mass of gas-charged ash, which is expelled with explosive force and moves hurricane speed down the mountainside.

Rockslides occur along a flat surface, usually when the layers of underlying rock are tilted at an angle, and are especially hazardous along road cuts.

Slides occur along flat or curved underground surfaces.

Slope stability encompasses the analysis of static and dynamic stability of slopes.

Slumps occur when material slides along a curved surface.

Solifluction occurs when the upper layers of soil become saturated and move downslope, common in very cold climates where permafrost forms. During the summer, the upper layer of the permafrost melts, saturating the ground and causing solifluction lobes.

Talus: A slope formed at the base of a steeper slope, made of fallen and disintegrated materials.

The Environment Calendar Days and Decades

(UNITED NATIONS)

Holocaust Day	January 27
World Wetland Day / Darwin's day	February 2
International Mother Language Day	February 21
National Science Day	February 28
International Women's Day	March 8
World Forestry Day	March 21
World Water day	March 22
World Meteorological Day	March 23
International Day for Mine Awareness and Assistance in Mine Action	April 4
World Health Day	April 7
World Heritage Day	April 18
Earth Day	April 22
World Information Society Day (Formerly World Telecommunication Day)	May 17
World Day for Cultural Diversity for Dialogue and Development	May 21
International Day for biological diversity	May 22
Anti Tobacco Day	May 31
World Environment Day	June 5
World Ocean Day	June 8
World Day to Combat Desertification and Drought	June 17

World Population Day	July 11
International Day of the World's Indigenous People	August 9
International Youth Day	August 12
International Literacy Day	September 8
International Day for the Preservation of the Ozone Layer	September 16
International Day of Peace (Formerly the opening day of the UN General Assembly, changed to a set date as of 2002)	September 21
Green Consumer Day	September 28
World Maritime Day	Last week of September
World Habitat Day	First Monday of October
World Animal Welfare Day	October 4
Wildlife week India	October 1 – 7
World Space Week	October 4 - 10
World Food Day	October 16
International Day for the Eradication of Poverty	October 17
United Nations Day	October 24
International Day for Natural Disaster Reduction	Second Wednesday of October
International Day for Preventing the Exploitation of the Environment in War and Armed Conflict	November 6
World AIDS Day	December 1
Human Rights Day	December 10
World Mountain Day	December 11
United Nations Decade for Women: Equality, Development and Peace	1976-1985
International Drinking Water Supply and Sanitation Decade	1981-1990

International Decade for Natural Disaster Reduction	1990-1999
International Decade of the World's Indigenous People	1994-2004
International Decade for a Culture of Peace and Non-Violence for the Children of the World	2001 - 2010
Decade to Roll Back Malaria in Developing Countries, Particularly in Africa	2001-2010
International Year of the Planet Earth	2008
United Nations Literacy Decade: Literacy for All	2003 – 2012
United Nations Decade of Education for Sustainable Development	2005 – 2014
International Decade for Action, "Water for Life"	2005 – 2015
United Nations Decade for Human Rights Education	1995- 2004

Some Important Environmental Conventions

Multilateral Environmental Agreements (MEAs) By The UNEP

Atmospheric Conventions

Vienna Convention for the Protection of the Ozone Layer	1985
Montreal Protocol on Substances that deplete the Ozone Layer	1987
United Nations Framework Convention on Climate Change	1992
Kyoto Protocol to the UN Framework Convention on Climate Change	1997

Biodiversity Conventions

Ramsar Convention on Wetlands	1971
World Heritage Convention	1972
Convention on International Trade in Endangered Species (CITES)	1973
Convention on Migratory Species (CMS)	1979
Convention on Biological Diversity	1992
Lusaka Agreement on Cooperative Enforcement Operations directed at Illegal Trade in Wild Fauna and Flora	1994
International Coral Reef Initiative (ICRI)	1995
Cartagena Protocol on Biosafety to the Convention on Biological Diversity	2001

Land Conventions

United Nations Convention to Combat Desertification	1992
Global Program of Action for the Protection of the Marine Environment From Land Based Activities	1995

Hazardous Wastes

Basel Convention on the Control of Transboundary Movements of Hazardous Wastes and their Disposal	1989
Basel Ban Amendment	1995
Basel Protocol on Liability and Compensation	1999
Future Stockholm Convention on Persistent Organic Pollutants	2001

Some important Acts and Notifications in India

1. The Motor Vehicle Act of 1938, amended in 1988
2. The Wildlife Protection Act, 1972, amended in 1983, 1986 and 1991.
3. The Water Prevention and Control of Pollution Act of 1974, amended

in 1991, which established the Central Pollution Control Board (CPCB) and State Pollution Control Boards (SPCB)

4. The Water Cess Act, 1977, amended in 1991

5. The Air Prevention and Control of Pollution Act of 1977 amended in 1981, 1988.

6. The Forest Conservation Act of 1980, amended in 1988

7. The Environment Protection Act of 1986

8. The Noise Pollution Act, 1987

9. The Hazardous Waste (Management and Handling) Rules, 1989 amended in 2000

10. The Manufacture, Storage and Import of Hazardous Chemicals Rules, 1989 amended in 2000

11. The Manufacture, Use, Import, Export and Storage of Hazardous Micro organisms or Cell Rules, 1989

12. The Public Liability Insurance Act of 1991

13. Notifications on the Coastal Regulation Zone, 1991

14. Notification on Environmental Statement, 1993

15. Environmental Impact Assessment of Development Projects, in 1994

16. Notification on Environmental Clearance, 1994

17. The National Environment Tribunal Act, 1995

18. The National Environment Appellate Authority Act, 1997.

REFERENCES

Abbott, Patrick L. 2004. Natural disasters. 4th ed. Boston, McGraw-Hill Higher Education.

Alexander, David. 2000. Confronting catastrophe: new perspectives on natural disasters. New York, Oxford University Press.

Allison, I. S. and Palmer, D. F. 1980. Geology, the science of a changing Earth. VII Edition. McGraw-Hill Inc.

Baskar S and Baskar R. 2007 Environmental Sciences for Engineering Undergraduates (First Edition) (As per AICTE notified syllabus) Unicorn Publishers, New Delhi.

Baskar S and Baskar R. 2007 Environmental Studies for Undergraduates (First Edition) (As per UGC notified syllabus) Unicorn Publishers, New Delhi.

Bryant, Edward. 2001. Tsunami: the underrated hazard. New York, Cambridge University Press.

Cesare Emiliani 1992. Planet Earth - Cosmology, geology and the evolution of life and the environment. Cambridge University press U.K.

Cox, K. G., Price, N. B. & Harte, B. 1974. An Introduction to the Practical Study of Crystals, Minerals and Rocks. Rev. Ist ed., John Wiley & Sons Inc., New York.

Davis, Lee. 2001. Natural disasters. Rev ed. New York, Facts on File, Inc.

Edward A. Keller. 2000. Environmental Geology (Eighth Edition). Prentice-Hall, Inc. New Jersey.

Erickson, Jon. 2001. Quakes, eruptions, and other geologic cataclysms: revealing the earth's hazards. Rev. ed. New York.

Hamilton, W. R., Woolley, A. R. and Bishop, A. C. 1984. The Hamlyn Guide to Minerals, Rocks and Fossils. The Hamlyn Publishing Group Ltd, London.

Lutgens, F.K and Tarbuck, E.J. 1998. Essentials of Geology. VI edition. Prentice Hall, Inc. New Jersey

Navalgund, R.R. 2001. Earth Observation Systems in Disaster management, presented at Special session ISPRS WG VII/4, Ahmedabad, 2001.

Nebel B.J. and Wright R.T. Environmental Science Prentice Hall Inc 1987.

Robinson, A.G. 2002. Earthshock: hurricanes, volcanoes, earthquakes, tornadoes, and other forces of nature. Rev. ed. New York, Thames & Hudson, 2002.

Smith, Keith. 2002. Environmental hazards: assessing risk and reducing disaster. 3rd ed. London, New York, Routledge.

Varnes D. J. 1978. Slope movement types and processes. In: Schuster R. L. & Krizek R. J. Ed., Landslides, analysis and control. Transportation Research Board Sp. Rep. No. 176, Nat. Acad. of Sciences, pp. 11-33, 1978.